I0017969

Apress Pocket Guides

Apress Pocket Guides present concise summaries of cutting-edge developments and working practices throughout the tech industry. Shorter in length, books in this series aims to deliver quick-to-read guides that are easy to absorb, perfect for the time-poor professional.

This series covers the full spectrum of topics relevant to the modern industry, from security, AI, machine learning, cloud computing, web development, product design, to programming techniques and business topics too.

Typical topics might include:

- A concise guide to a particular topic, method, function or framework

- Professional best practices and industry trends

- A snapshot of a hot or emerging topic

- Industry case studies

- Concise presentations of core concepts suited for students and those interested in entering the tech industry

- Short reference guides outlining 'need-to-know' concepts and practices.

More information about this series at https://link.springer.com/ bookseries/17385.

From Culture to Code

Leading Software Engineering
Teams Effectively

Jonathan Sosa

Apress®

From Culture to Code: Leading Software Engineering Teams Effectively

Jonathan Sosa
Tokyo, Japan

ISBN-13 (pbk): 979-8-8688-1427-3   ISBN-13 (electronic): 979-8-8688-1428-0
https://doi.org/10.1007/979-8-8688-1428-0

Managing Director, Apress Media LLC: Welmoed Spahr
Acquisitions Editor: Shivangi Ramachandran
Development Editor: James Markham
Editorial Assistant: Jessica Vakkili

Cover designed by eStudioCalamar

Cover image designed by Freepik (www.freepik.com)

Distributed to the book trade worldwide by Springer Science+Business Media New York, 1 New York Plaza, New York, NY 10004. Phone 1-800-SPRINGER, fax (201) 348-4505, e-mail orders-ny@springer-sbm.com, or visit www.springeronline.com. Apress Media, LLC is a Delaware LLC and the sole member (owner) is Springer Science + Business Media Finance Inc (SSBM Finance Inc). SSBM Finance Inc is a **Delaware** corporation.

For information on translations, please e-mail booktranslations@springernature.com; for reprint, paperback, or audio rights, please e-mail bookpermissions@springernature.com.

Apress titles may be purchased in bulk for academic, corporate, or promotional use. eBook versions and licenses are also available for most titles. For more information, reference our Print and eBook Bulk Sales web page at http://www.apress.com/bulk-sales.

Any source code or other supplementary material referenced by the author in this book is available to readers on GitHub. For more detailed information, please visit https://www.apress.com/gp/services/source-code.

If disposing of this product, please recycle the paper

To the women who shaped who I am today:
my grandmother, my mother, my wife, and
my baby daughter.

Table of Contents

About the Author xiii

Acknowledgments xv

Prologue xvii

Introduction xxi

Chapter 1: Develop Your Presence...1

    Become a Role Model 2

        Have Impeccable Integrity 3

        Keep Your Words and Actions in Check 4

        Assume Ownership of Almost Everything.......................6

    Formulate a Vision for Your Team.......................................7

    Expand Your Influence..8

        Offer Value 9

        Volunteer Strategically 10

    Make Difficult Decisions 11

    Key Points 13

Chapter 2: Champion Your Team...15

    Revisit Your Organization's Policies 16

    Give Your Team the Tools to Succeed 17

    Recognize Your Team's Accomplishments 18

    Help Your Team Navigate Tough Times...........................19

        Remain Calm 20

Acknowledge the Challenge 20

Come Up with a Plan 21

Celebrate Small Victories 21

Key Points 22

Chapter 3: Acquire Talent **23**

Write Effective Job Descriptions 24

Introduction of the Organization, the Team, and Why You Are Hiring 24

Expectations Toward This Position 25

Required Skills and Qualifications 25

Nice-to-Haves 26

Additional Information 26

Attract Potential Candidates 27

Publish an Engineering Blog 27

Contribute to Open Source Projects 27

Speak at Events 28

Sponsor 28

Set Up the Hiring Pipeline 29

Resume Screening 30

Technical Screening 30

Culture Fit Interview 31

Hiring Manager Interview 31

Senior Leadership Interview 31

Interview and Assess 32

Hire Candidates 34

Onboard New Hires 36

Team Onboarding Documentation 36

Repository README...37

Mentor Support..37

Bring in External Help When Necessary...38

Key Points 39

Chapter 4: Organize Your People 41

Form Teams by Function or by Project...41

Consider the Team Topologies Framework 43

Stream-Aligned Teams 44

Enabling Teams 44

Complicated Subsystem Teams...44

Platform Teams..44

Reduce Cognitive Load and Cross-Team Interactions............................45

Choose the Right Engineering Managers...45

Key Points 47

Chapter 5: Set Expectations and Evaluate Against Them 49

Define an Engineering Ladder...50

Junior Engineer 52

Intermediate Engineer 52

Senior Engineer 53

Staff Engineer..53

Principal Engineer 54

Decide the Frequency of Evaluations..55

Prepare Evaluations 56

Deliver Evaluation Results 57

Promote High Performers 59

Deal with Underperformers..61

Lack of Understanding of Expectations 61

Lack of Skills 62

Personal Issues 62

Lack of Desire to Contribute 63

Key Points 64

Chapter 6: Set Goals **65**

Define Team OKRs..66

Define Objectives...66

Define Key Results..66

Keep Track of Team OKRs 68

Consider Introducing Personal OKRs 69

Avoid Using OKRs in Performance Evaluations 69

Key Points 70

Chapter 7: Deliver Impactful Projects................................**73**

Know What to Build..74

Business Motivation 74

Constraints 74

Assign Roles and Responsibilities 75

Define an Escalation Protocol 76

Manage Complexity 77

Help Manage the Backlog 79

Key Points 80

Chapter 8: Adopt Best Practices.......................................**83**

Decide How "Agile" You Want to Be 83

Common Agile Pitfalls..85

Use a Task Management Tool 86

Define Code Review Guidelines 88

Define Communication Guidelines 89

    Meetings 89

    Online Messaging 91

    Communication in Multicultural Environments 93

Key Points 94

Chapter 9: Build Software Right **95**

Choose the Tech Stack 96

    Multiplatform Frameworks 98

Don't Use Prototypes As a Starting Point 100

Set Coding Standards 100

Configure Continuous Integration, Continuous Delivery (CI/CD) 102

Start with the Building Blocks 103

    UI Components 104

    API Clients 104

    State Management 105

    Error Handling 105

    Observability 105

Manage Technical Debt 106

    Pay Off Technical Debt 107

    Rewriting from Scratch 109

Key Points 110

Chapter 10: Choose Quality **113**

Limit Your Commitments 114

    Publicize What You're Working On 115

    Focus on One Big Thing per Day 116

    Schedule Your Work 117

Avoid Unreasonable Deadlines...117

Eat Your Own Dog Food...119

Key Points 120

Chapter 11: Take Care of Yourself....................................121

Chapter 12: Closing Words 125

Bibliography 127

About the Author

 **Jonathan Sosa** is a seasoned engineering leader with two decades of experience delivering software used by millions worldwide. He currently serves as the Head of Engineering at Foundation LLM Technologies, Inc., a pioneering Silicon Valley startup developing AI tools for design and manufacturing. Previously, Jonathan served as VP of Engineering at Drivemode Inc., Honda's software innovation arm, where he spearheaded the development of a groundbreaking In-Vehicle Infotainment and Companion Apps platform for Honda's electric vehicles. Before his tenure at Drivemode, Jonathan was a Director of Engineering at Mercari, Inc., Japan's first unicorn. There, he led the team behind Mercari's mobile and web applications tailored for the US market. Jonathan also held the position of Group Manager at Rakuten, where he led the Digital Content Platform Development Group. Additionally, he played a pivotal role in shaping the success of multiple Japanese tech startups. A Computer Science honors graduate from the Tecnológico de Monterrey, Jonathan speaks five languages, holds a US patent, and is certified as an Agile Product Owner and Scrum Master.

Acknowledgments

I don't think it's possible to thank all the people who have contributed, directly or indirectly, to the making of this book, but let me name a few.

I consider myself incredibly lucky to be surrounded by inspiring leaders from whom I've learned a lot over the years. I'm particularly grateful to those who kindly reviewed the early drafts of this manuscript: Ken Wakasa, Maho Aragon, and Mok Oh. Their incredibly helpful feedback helped shape the content of this book.

Having worked at Rakuten Kobo, the digital reading company, I was a little familiar with book publishing, but I had never written a book myself. I want to thank Shivangi Ramachandran, Krishnan Sathyamurthy, Jessica Vakili, James Markham, and the rest of the Apress team for believing in this project and holding my hand through the entire process. It's been a pleasure working with you.

Thanks to the many bosses, colleagues, and clients for their patience, trust, and support during my career so far. Some of them are no longer with us, but they are never forgotten.

I also thank all my family, teachers, and friends, who don't have much to do with software engineering but have been a huge influence on my life. And, of course, to my wife Kaori, who, while being pregnant with our baby daughter, gave me so much support and encouragement during the writing process.

Prologue

I've been fascinated by computers since I first met the original Macintosh when I was seven, back in the mid-1980s. I can't recall much of my childhood, but I vividly remember when my aunt taught me to play a game named *Dark Castle* on this mysterious beige box at her office. *It's like a TV, but you can control what happens on the screen?!*

My aunt was an executive assistant at a private college, the Tecnológico de Monterrey—the same college I graduated from 14 years later. My grandfather would pick her up after work, and he would take me with him. I was always excited to play for a few minutes on her computer while she was getting ready to leave work.

My parents were never interested in computers or video games, so convincing them to buy them for me was always a struggle. I got the Atari 2600 after a year of begging, right at the end of its lifespan. The following year, I asked for a Nintendo console for Christmas but got a bicycle instead. I know they were trying to get me to play outside, but I only rode that bicycle three times.

Fast-forward to the early 1990s. I was lucky to get a scholarship to Eugenio Garza Lagüera, a high school operated by the Tecnológico de Monterrey. On my first day, my mom drove me, and I remember glancing out the car window at a student selling used 3.5-inch floppy disks—the ones you still see on the Save menu on Word and Excel.

I immediately joined the computer club. We had perks like advanced computer lessons and access to an exclusive room with NeXT computers. In exchange, we volunteered to mentor and offer technical support to other students using the computers at school. I chose Saturday mornings as my shift; it was quiet, and I had plenty of time to mess around.

My first experience with programming was HyperTalk on a Macintosh SE/30—still beige. HyperTalk was a scripting language used to program interactive elements in HyperCard, an application based on the concept of a stack of virtual cards. How these cards worked inspired the creation of hyperlinks, the HTTP protocol, and JavaScript.

I spent all my free time in a computer room or at the soccer field. I had good friends but never hung out at the cafeteria or outside school. I was always doing something.

I graduated high school with honors and got a college scholarship. I was very thankful because my parents couldn't afford such an expensive tuition. I chose Computer Science as my major and French as my minor. I was also interested in marketing, but the decision was easy.

I've never considered myself particularly intelligent, but I'm incredibly industrious. I won't rest until I get it done. I also liked getting good grades. I figured, why not do the best I can if time is going to pass anyway?

I was also curious. I think computer science is a good career choice for curious people. It has both depth and breadth: You can use software to solve problems across almost all industries, and to understand the problem, you need to familiarize yourself with it. Are you developing an ecommerce website? You learn about marketing, financial transactions, and shipping logistics. A car navigation system? You learn about GPS, vehicle safety, and road regulations.

In my first year of college, I had a summer job at my old high school, implementing a student management web application. My team and I were using WebObjects, a web framework initially developed by Steve Jobs at NeXT, which he later brought to Apple to use as the base for Xcode.

It was a fun summer job. We had Macintosh, Windows, NeXT, Linux, and even BeOS machines. I learned a lot from my teammates, all of whom were hired by Apple a few years later to build the Apple online store. Over the years, they invited me to interview at Apple multiple times, but they finally gave up after realizing I would not leave Japan.

In my second year, I switched from French to Japanese and was invited to help manage the school's anime club. In the mid-1990s, computers were often associated with video games, anime, and comic subcultures, and I didn't mind being a nerd.

Around this time, I was trying to do all my homework assignments on Macintosh while almost everyone else was doing them on Windows. Back then, Mac OS 7 (a.k.a. "System 7") was very unstable; I remember getting the infamous "bomb" system error message a few times a day. My classmates sometimes made fun of me when I presented my work on a Macintosh. It's funny how different things are now that Macs are everywhere, and having a Windows computer is seen as uncool.

There came a point when the assignments were impossible on MacOS: flashing assembly code to a microcontroller, implementing a game's AI in Scheme, building a custom compiler in Visual Basic, etc. So, I was forced to switch to Windows. The upside was that I could spend more time with my friends, who were all in the Windows computer room. We played a lot of *Warcraft* and *Starcraft*, yes, the first versions.

In my last year, I had so much schoolwork that my parents finally bought me my first computer, precisely speaking, the parts of it, and I assembled it. I felt like a miracle when I turned it on for the first time. Computer science students were all assembling their computers; it was cheaper, and you could put into practice what you learned at school.

I graduated at 21 from college during the dot-com bubble era and got a good corporate job at FEMSA, a Latin-American conglomerate. I had my own office and reported directly to an executive officer. Computer science was in high demand, and there weren't many of us.

I was set up for a good career, but I knew I wanted something else— I used almost all my salary to repay my student loan as soon as possible, and I got yet another scholarship, this time to study in Japan. I moved in the early 2000s, and I've been in Tokyo since then.

Introduction

This book synthesizes my 20 years of experience building and leading software engineering teams across real estate, digital reading, ecommerce, automotive, and AI industries. It encompasses not only my insights but also the collective wisdom of other engineering leaders I've had the privilege to work with, lessons from countless books and training sessions, and, most importantly, practical knowledge gained from writing a lot of software myself.

Throughout the book, when I use the term "leadership," I refer to a position with managerial authority, such as engineering manager, director of engineering, VP of engineering, or CTO. While leadership is certainly not confined to these roles and can be demonstrated at any level, I focus on offering ideas relevant to roles with explicit responsibilities for team and organizational outcomes.

I wrote this book with the insights I wish I had known when I first stepped into a senior leadership role. Back in 2009, I became the CTO of a small startup in the west of Japan called Zenkei. We were working on the early VR and AR technology for real estate companies. Although I was technically the strongest individual contributor, I didn't have the experience to manage people, let alone being the CTO. The CEO did his best to mentor me, but he didn't have a software engineering background.

I remember that what I struggled with the most was dealing with ambiguity. Regardless of the industry, in leadership roles, there is rarely a clear-cut directive or a step-by-step guide to follow. Nobody would tell me exactly what to do, so I had to learn quickly to make decisions based on limited information and unclear paths.

Since then, I've led software engineering teams in organizations at different stages of maturity, from well-established tech companies to fast-growing startups, including the very first Japanese unicorn, Mercari. I have also served as an advisor for various companies, mentoring their engineers and helping them deliver successful software. In every engagement, I had the opportunity to learn something about leadership, sometimes by observing, but most of the time by trying things myself.

At the time of this writing, I serve as Head of Engineering for a Silicon Valley startup that builds AI tools for design and manufacturing and I'm happy to say that I get to work with people I admire.

I don't presume my ideas and insights are exhaustive or infallible. Instead, consider them as a foundational starting point. It is up to you to understand them, experiment with them, and find out what works for you. I'm sure you'll encounter ideas that don't resonate with your situation when you read them. I expect that. I ask you not to discard them immediately and give them a chance a few months later. Perhaps they'll spark something, then.

This book has a mix of soft skills and hard technical skills. I believe both are important. Good leaders can *walk the talk*, give concrete and practical guidance to their teams, and even make code contributions in strategic areas when necessary. You could get away with having only soft skills for a while by attending meetings and telling people what to do, but I've noticed that's not enough to gain genuine respect and admiration from engineers.

My writing style is compact and to the point—it tries to deliver the essence and nothing else. I didn't want to add content to reach a word count quota. You'll notice that most sentences are simple and short; please read them carefully and reflect on how they relate to you.

I must confess that I used Grammarly, an AI-powered writing aid, to polish my writing. English is not my mother tongue, so I needed some extra help. At first, it felt like I was cheating, but I realized that nowadays, everyone uses AI tools to aid with content creation. The cat is out of the box and never going back. In my opinion, using AI tools is okay if they don't dissolve your personality. AI tends to go for what's widely accepted as "correct." If I had let Grammarly apply all of its suggestions, I would have ended up with a very bland book.

I sincerely hope you find this resource helpful in growing as an engineering leader.

CHAPTER 1

Develop Your Presence

As an engineering leader, your scope extends beyond your technical domain. You must address challenges outside your immediate vicinity and demonstrate confidence that transcends technical expertise. You're expected to inspire trust, make difficult decisions, and drive success.

If you recently stepped into this role, you'll have to let go of deep day-to-day engagement and stop trying to solve every problem on your own, no matter how good you are at it. You're no longer an individual contributor. Instead, empower others and ensure they grow and contribute to the organization's goals.

This transition wasn't evident to me. Initially, I spent too much time writing code and debugging issues myself instead of delegating. I figured I could do something faster than asking someone else since I knew how. This mentality has two problems: first, it's not scalable—you can't do everything yourself—and second, it deprives your team of learning opportunities.

As Scott Eblin writes in his book *The Next Level: What Insiders Know About Executive Success*: "You reach that point when the scope of the role gets to be so big that you can't successfully continue as the hero or heroine who always scores the goal. To be successful at the next level, you have to let go of being the go-to person and pick up being the leader who builds teams of go-to people."

© Jonathan Sosa 2025
J. Sosa, *From Culture to Code*, Apress Pocket Guides,
https://doi.org/10.1007/979-8-8688-1428-0_1

When you delegate, you remove tasks from your to-do list that your team can execute for you. This gives you more time to focus on things only you can do. And gives your team opportunities to learn and grow.

In essence, your efforts as a senior leader should focus on these key areas:

- Defining a vision and goals

- Setting expectations and holding people accountable

- Building, growing, and organizing your teams

- Adopting and enforcing best practices systematically

- Delivering quality software

If you're spending too much time on individual tasks that don't contribute meaningfully to these core areas, consider taking a step back to reassess your day-to-day. I will give you plenty of ideas on what to focus on.

Become a Role Model

Whether you like it or not, people will look up to you for inspiration, direction, and guidance. They will view your words and actions as benchmarks for their own performance and professional development. This influence carries significant responsibility, as the way you carry yourself can profoundly change team morale, motivation, and, ultimately, impact.

Being a good role model isn't something you can simply declare for yourself—it's a status granted by others based on their perception of you. It's earned through consistent integrity and the ability to lead by example in both ordinary and difficult situations. People judge you by observing how well your actions align with your words and how you treat others.

Needless to say, this perception is very fragile. One minor slipup can ruin your reputation, diminish your credibility, and overshadow the positive impact you've worked so hard to create. Losing your temper and screaming at someone, not keeping up your commitments, or lying can throw years of work down the drain. Trust is the most powerful tool you have, and without it, people won't follow you.

Imagine your boss abuses their position of power to use the company budget on personal expenses. Would you trust them with your career? Would you follow their lead? Would you even listen seriously to what they have to say? Of course not. They lost your trust and respect.

I've been very lucky to have a few role models in my career. Individuals that I looked up to. They all had different strengths and weaknesses; I never expected them to be perfect or know it all, but they all share a few common attributes: they have impeccable integrity, are always calm and respectful, and assume ownership of almost everything.

Have Impeccable Integrity

First and foremost, maintain impeccable integrity. Show respect for the organization, its people, its rules, and its policies. I've met leaders who think the rules don't apply to them due to their seniority; needless to say, they are wrong, and surely enough, I saw them lose the respect of the people around them.

In the course of your career, you'll encounter loopholes or "gray zones" where you could get away with something that formally doesn't break the rules but has an ethically questionable angle. While it might be tempting to justify such decisions by pointing to the absence of explicit prohibitions, I suggest you always take the safe side. If you find yourself questioning whether something is right, it's often a sign to refrain from proceeding. When in doubt, don't do it.

Borrowing from Harvard Business Review's *Manager's Handbook*: "What makes ethics so difficult is that not everyone has the same rules; our ethical compasses have been conditioned by our upbringing, our education, and the behavior we observe around us. You ultimately need to have your own compass for ethical issues. The fact that someone in your company tells you something is ethical doesn't make it so."

A leader is constantly scrutinized and talked about behind closed doors on private channels and DMs. Don't give anyone additional reasons to criticize you. The more you do, the more you weaken your authority—Why should your subordinates respect the rules and be ethical if you aren't?

Integrity also entails honesty in all your words and actions. Don't lie or pretend to be something you're not. If you don't know something, admit it; it's okay. I know this might be particularly hard for new leaders coming from a purely technical background, as they were expected always to have answers to technical problems.

In a leadership position, nobody expects you to be perfect or know it all. *"I'm sorry, I don't know, but I'll figure it out"* is one of my favorite phrases. In my experience, people appreciate honesty much more than knowledge or expertise.

Additionally, demonstrate integrity by upholding your commitments. If you make a promise, ensure you follow through. Don't say yes and take on more than you can handle just to please someone or get them off your back. If I ask an engineer to look into an issue and they say they will but don't actually do it, I'll doubt their words next time. Naturally, I won't be able to rely on them for critical work going forward. I prefer they decline my request from the start so I can find someone else who can take it.

Keep Your Words and Actions in Check

Given your influential role, you don't have the luxury of complaining or being visibly frustrated. People are always watching how you conduct yourself during meetings, working at your desk, or even taking a break.

Once, one of my engineers caught me venting to my boss in the men's bathroom after a long day—it was a stark reminder that every action and expression can negatively affect others.

While it's natural to experience negative emotions, it's important to manage and avoid displaying them in professional settings, not only in the office but also in online meetings and team gatherings outside of work. Always try to preserve composure, positivity, and calmness.

That being said, no matter how hard you work to control your feelings, you'll probably have moments when you can't contain them—for example, lashing out at a colleague or verbalizing frustration during a difficult conversation. Leaders are also humans. Forgive yourself, take the time to recognize what is happening, and apologize to the involved parties.

Also, keep your sense of humor in check. Avoid sarcasm and irony. Don't joke about performance, compensation, or personal issues, no matter how innocent you think it might be. These types of jokes are not only unfunny but can create awkward situations at best and, at worst, potentially violate workplace compliance guidelines. I've been lucky to work on international teams over the past decade, but some cultural differences can be surprising for someone who hasn't.

Your words have a lot of weight, and they might cause misunderstandings, hurt feelings, or damage trust within your team. While humor can effectively build rapport and alleviate stress, it must be used appropriately. Inappropriate jokes or offhand remarks can create an uncomfortable environment.

If your workplace offers compliance training, I encourage you to use it. Even if you're confident in the integrity and professionalism of your communication, you might be surprised by what you learn. Compliance training highlights nuances in workplace policies, cultural sensitivities, and legal guidelines that may not be immediately obvious.

Assume Ownership of Almost Everything

As you rise in the organization's ranks, you lose the right to say, "That's not my job." It's no longer acceptable to point your finger at others, complain, or ignore issues that you have the power to solve. There is almost always something you can do to make things better. You have resources, authority, and, hopefully, a strong influence to leverage.

For example, if someone in your team is not performing as expected, ask yourself how you contributed to it. What are some things you could have done to support them better? What tools could you have offered them? Did you make their expectations clear? Did you put them on the right team? You get the point. Realizing that the fault will never be completely on their side and that you share a percentage of it can help you improve the situation.

The same can be said for problems outside of your team. If the sales team couldn't land that big client, ask yourself what deficiencies in the product your team developed contributed to it. Perhaps they could have closed the contract if you had delivered that extra feature or if it had fewer bugs. Again, a small part of it was your fault.

This mindset encourages individuals, especially those in higher positions, to take full responsibility for their organization's performance and outcomes. Goals are often interconnected, and everyone can contribute to them.

Furthermore, when you demonstrate a commitment to ownership, you set an example for others. It helps create a culture where everyone feels accountable for not just their own work but also for the collective success. It pushes people to step up and help each other.

Formulate a Vision for Your Team

A compelling vision is necessary not only to inspire and guide your team toward a shared purpose but also to ensure its alignment with the organization. It is your responsibility to lead the formulation of such a vision.

Begin by collaborating with fellow leaders to identify your organization's core values and overarching goals. Your vision should not exist in isolation. It should be aligned with the rest of the organization. Otherwise, you'll have trouble getting resources and coordinating efforts across different teams.

Then, ask yourself and your team "What do we want to become?" or "Where do we want to go?" and work backward from that to create some vision drafts. Use concise, inclusive, and impactful language that resonates with as many people as possible. Avoid jargon—they can get intimidated and not want to tell you they didn't understand.

For example, if your team builds ecommerce websites, a potential vision could be: "We are a world-class engineering team that delivers high-quality, delightful ecommerce websites."

Once you and your team have finalized and agreed upon the vision, share it with the rest of the organization. Publish the vision internally so that all team members and stakeholders know your team's goals and aspirations. External stakeholders, such as other departments, partners, or clients, should also be informed about what your team is aiming for.

Having a vision on paper is just the beginning; the real challenge lies in having your team internalize it. This is where things get difficult. Interestingly, despite all the management and leadership books I've read, few—if any—offer details on how to make a vision part of the team's culture. I believe this is because a vision is intrinsically vague.

The key is to crystalize it into something more tangible, concrete, and actionable through engineering goals. Going back to the vision, "We are a world-class engineering team that delivers high-quality, delightful ecommerce websites," I would add goals that support it, like "Our websites have an average Net Promoter Score of 45 or more." And, of course, recognize and reward engineers who contribute toward that goal.

I also suggest revisiting your vision every few months to verify it's still relevant and aligned with the rest of the organization. Many factors might suggest an update, such as pivoting to a different product or service or changing industry trends. Or perhaps your team has evolved, and you need a more ambitious vision.

Expand Your Influence

The authority granted by your official title is your primary source of influence. The organization has handed you a sword that you can use to direct your people and enforce the rules. However, there are two limitations to relying only on this type of influence.

- Authority is limited in scope: It typically applies only to your direct reports. However, to be an effective leader, your influence must extend in all directions—upward to your superiors, laterally to your peers, and outward to other organizational stakeholders. Without this broader reach, your leadership impact is confined and less effective in driving collaboration and alignment across the board.

- Authority doesn't inspire or motivate: When people follow commands solely because they are obligated to, their engagement is transactional and lacks the emotional commitment needed for top performance. Engineers may comply with your orders, but genuine passion is sparked when they feel inspired by a leader they respect and trust.

Expand your influence beyond the boundaries of your formal authority by investing in meaningful relationships with those around you. Be careful, though; faking interest in others or operating with a hidden agenda is counterproductive. People are often perceptive and can sense someone's intentions aren't sincere. When you aren't genuine, it undermines trust and can damage relationships rather than build them. Authenticity is key.

While formal authority gives you the power to direct and enforce, true leadership comes from your ability to influence without relying on your title. Below are some ideas on how to expand your influence.

Offer Value

Focusing on how to offer value to others has worked well for me. I'm not extroverted, so trying to bond with someone over personal life or hobbies doesn't come naturally to me. Instead, I try to figure out how to be of service, help them look good, or even reach a goal.

Offering something of value tends to trigger an urge in the other person to reciprocate. Reciprocity is a social and psychological principle where people feel obligated to return a favor or respond in kind when someone does something for them. It is a fundamental aspect of human interaction. A socially well-adjusted person will undoubtedly try to offer you something in return later on.

Note that this doesn't mean the relationship should be transactional. Avoid falling into the mindset of, "I did this for you, so now you must do that for me." Relationships built on such a tit-for-tat foundation often lack depth and genuine connection.

Offering value to others doesn't necessarily require grand or extravagant gestures. Often, the small, thoughtful actions make the most significant impact. Simple acts like helping to proofread a report, recommending a great restaurant, or giving public praise are greatly appreciated. These gestures may seem minor, but they strengthen relationships.

Evidently, the best way to offer value to your superiors is to do your job effectively and deliver results. As a bonus, I suggest you always share credit. For instance, if someone praised you for successfully completing a project, you might respond with something like, "I couldn't have done it without your guidance and support." Even if they didn't play a direct role in your achievement, I'm sure they did indirectly. You should make them feel like they contributed. Next time, they'll feel the urge to help you more proactively.

Volunteer Strategically

Beyond your official responsibilities, you'll encounter opportunities to volunteer and contribute in various ways within your organization. While taking on all these opportunities to showcase your commitment might be tempting, doing so can quickly lead to burnout. It's important to recognize that you have limited time and energy, and overcommitting can negatively impact your primary duties and personal well-being.

However, when chosen wisely, some of these volunteering opportunities can be valuable investments that help expand your influence. Strategic volunteering involves selecting initiatives that benefit the organization and contribute to your growth as a leader. For example, volunteering to lead a high-visibility project can showcase your skills and open doors. Participating in cross-departmental committees can broaden your understanding of the organization and build relationships with peers in other areas.

Engaging in speaking events enhances your reputation within and outside the organization. Sharing your expertise and experiences not only contributes to the collective knowledge of your peers but also positions you as an authority in your field.

I often volunteer to mentor new hires who will eventually become my peers or even my superiors. By establishing these relationships early, I foster a sense of mutual respect and get an opportunity to influence someone on a different team. Colleagues I've mentored are forever grateful and more than willing to help me when I need them. You never know how far they can grow and advance their careers in the organization.

In recent years, I have had the privilege of welcoming and mentoring a new Director of Product and a new Director of Technical Program Management (TPM) in the companies I worked for. Although these positions do not fall directly under the engineering department, they are nonetheless critical to the organization's success.

During our mentoring sessions, I shared insights into the organizational challenges from an engineering perspective and discussed ways our departments can collaborate better. As you can probably imagine, these discussions significantly influenced the prioritization of their efforts during their first few months at the company as they worked to earn the trust and respect of people around them.

The relationship we built stayed strong after the mentoring period was over. We continued to have regular one-on-ones and worked on ideas on how to improve our interteam synergies. For example, the Director of TPM and I outlined a team structure where every major project would have a dedicated TPM assigned to it. TPMs took some of the workload that was burdening engineers: road map planning, milestone tracking, and progress reporting.

Make Difficult Decisions

Unfortunately, decision-making often falls into extreme categories, portraying every choice as a success or a failure. This kind of black-and-white thinking generates unnecessary stress and is simply not productive.

Not all your decisions need to be correct. In fact, most often exist in shades of gray rather than clear-cut right or wrong choices, especially in complex situations. Sometimes, it will feel like you have to pick between two bad options. For instance, you might have to decide between allocating limited resources to a project with high potential but significant risks versus a safer initiative with guaranteed but modest returns. Both options have their pros and cons.

As Janice Fraser suggests in her excellent book *Farther, Faster, and Far Less Drama: How to Reduce Stress and Make Extraordinary Progress Wherever You Lead*, replace the question "Is this the right thing to do?" with "Is this something we could all live with?" to alleviate some of the decision-making pressure. The goal is to make good enough decisions and move forward.

It should be sufficient if everyone can live with the decision, even if they don't entirely agree that it's the "right" one. Striving for consensus is usually wasteful and unnecessary and I would say impossible in most difficult decisions related to software engineering. Instead, focus on reaching one that all stakeholders can get behind.

On the other hand, when someone objects by saying they can't live with the decision, it signifies a major concern, which should trigger a reevaluation of the options. Don't ignore objections—Even if they make you postpone the decision, they might save you trouble, perhaps a catastrophe down the line. Maybe the individual who's objecting knows something you don't. Listen.

To make a well-informed decision, you need the input of two groups of people: those with expertise on the matter and those who have to live with the decision's outcome. The first group has the knowledge and insights needed to educate the decision-makers. The second group can foresee the consequences better than anyone else. Failing to include both groups will likely result in decisions that don't stick.

Decisions that don't stick are worse than indecision because they are difficult to detect. Some stakeholders will be quiet and secretly disagree; others will pretend to agree but won't follow through or put in effort. I've seen this happening more often in large organizations, where it's generally easier to conceal. A lot of time could be wasted before you realize that you need to go back, engage, and try again to reach a decision.

I've found that the best way to prevent secret disagreements is to have a conversation privately with each stakeholder and ask for their thoughts. Approach them from a place of vulnerability and genuine interest in their opinions, opening the conversation with something along the lines of "I need your advice about the matter. Do you have a few minutes this week?"

Key Points

- Leaders must shift from hands-on problem-solving to empowering teams, defining visions, and driving organizational goals.

- Leadership is judged by behavior, consistency, and ability to inspire trust. Integrity is nonnegotiable.

- A clear, inspiring vision aligned with organizational goals guides teams effectively.

- Influence extends beyond formal authority; it is built upon relationships.

- Effective leaders make "livable" decisions rather than seeking perfect ones.

CHAPTER 2

Champion Your Team

As a leader, you are in a challenging position: you represent both the organization's interests and those of your team members. While you should attempt to reconcile these interests, there will inevitably be situations where they oppose one another entirely, requiring you to choose a side. Balancing these responsibilities requires diplomacy, empathy, and a deep understanding of both organizational goals and your team member's needs.

I've found that in the long term, it pays off to prioritize your team members. It builds trust and respect with them, which you can leverage to boost morale and performance. When team members feel valued and supported, they are more motivated to contribute, take initiative, and commit to their work. So, the organization ends up benefiting too. Organizational priorities and direction change, but people stay.

Naturally, this assumes that all team members act with integrity and respect the organization's rules and policies. If someone doesn't, prioritize the organization's well-being and address the situation promptly. In nearly every workplace, there are individuals who will attempt to abuse the system by exploiting loopholes, taking shortcuts, or misusing resources for personal gain. It is your responsibility to monitor, confront, and resolve such behavior. If you don't, others will follow a similar pattern.

© Jonathan Sosa 2025
J. Sosa, *From Culture to Code*, Apress Pocket Guides,
https://doi.org/10.1007/979-8-8688-1428-0_2

Revisit Your Organization's Policies

After compensation and career growth, I've found that one of the most valued aspects for engineers is freedom, specifically the flexibility to choose what to work on, when, and where to work. When engineers have the freedom to select work that aligns with their interests and strengths, they are more likely to engage deeply, leading to increased innovation. Remote work options further contribute to this flexibility, enabling engineers to work from environments where they feel most comfortable and productive.

The level of freedom engineers have is fundamentally shaped by the organization's policies. These policies govern critical aspects such as work hours, remote work allowance, project assignments, and overall autonomy in how engineers approach their tasks. Typically, these policies are formulated during the early stages of an organization, often without feedback from the engineering team. As a result, they may not address engineers' unique needs, preferences, and working styles, potentially restricting their flexibility and impacting their overall job satisfaction.

Therefore, as an advocate for your engineering team, you should take proactive steps to influence and shape organizational policies to serve your team's interests better. This involves actively seeking opportunities to provide feedback, presenting data-driven arguments highlighting the benefits of increased flexibility, and collaborating with management and Human Resources to implement policy adjustments.

A good way to approach controversial changes is to introduce time-bounded pilot programs. For example, you could introduce a work-from-home pilot for a month while tracking productivity metrics like story points, features, or pull requests delivered. Monitor and analyze these metrics throughout the pilot to assess the change's impact. After the pilot period, present the results to Human Resources and relevant stakeholders. The policy can be permanently adopted if the outcomes have a positive effect.

Give Your Team the Tools to Succeed

Equipping engineers with the necessary tools, such as high-end computers, is essential for their success. I've observed organizations with strict budget policies attempting to cut costs by providing low-end computers, ultimately reducing productivity. Often, nontechnical managers make these decisions without a clear understanding of the engineers' needs. This mismatch not only causes inefficiencies and frustration but also undermines the overall effectiveness of the team. Step in, negotiate, and get what your engineers need to succeed.

Besides hardware equipment, software tools are crucial in empowering engineering teams to perform at their best. Today, countless offerings are designed to automate tasks and save engineers' time, allowing them to focus on more complex aspects of their work. These tools range from QA automation to advanced AI copilots, each serving a specific purpose to enhance efficiency.

Choosing the right tool is a team effort that should consider members' needs and preferences, the projects' requirements, and the existing workflows and infrastructure. It is also important to evaluate how well the tool integrates with the current tech stack. Additionally, you should assess factors such as ease of use, security, scalability, cost-effectiveness, and the availability of support resources. It will be a long-term relationship. Take the time upfront to ensure it's the right one.

Tools for training and education are also essential for developing your team's skills and keeping them up to date with the latest technologies and industry practices. Consider getting an enterprise subscription for a learning platform like Coursera or Udemy. These platforms offer a vast array of courses, tutorials, and resources covering various topics relevant to software engineering and leadership. Work with your organization to set an education budget to cover these costs.

I suggest constantly collecting feedback regarding their available equipment and tools. Regularly soliciting input through surveys, one-on-one meetings, or team discussions helps identify shortcomings. Some engineers tend to stay quiet, so you have to ask them explicitly.

If the input indicates insufficient tooling, compile and present a case to justify the additional budget allocation, highlighting the impact on performance and overall team morale.

Recognize Your Team's Accomplishments

Publicly recognizing successes, both big and small, reinforces a sense of achievement and validates each team member's hard work and dedication. It makes them feel valued and appreciated, increasing morale and motivation.

This recognition makes individuals want to work with you. You should constantly look for opportunities to celebrate and give credit. For example, you can highlight recent achievements in team meetings, retrospectives, and organization-wide all-hands. Remember to be specific and mention everyone involved, who did what, and how it positively impacted the organization. Take the time to prepare your speech, and don't forget anyone who participated in the effort.

I'm a fan of publicizing promotions. While a promotion is a form of recognition all by itself, why not amplify it and make it an event? Besides, the rest of the organization should be aware of the newly promoted individual's added responsibilities so they can raise their expectations accordingly.

I know that in some places, promotions are kept private to avoid potential feelings of envy among those who didn't get them. But this shouldn't be a concern if the promotion is well-earned and you have a good team culture. If you feel this is not the case, you have work to do: start fostering an environment where engineers celebrate each other's successes.

You can also work with your Human Resources representative to implement formal recognition programs, such as achievement awards or peer-nominated accolades. These programs provide structured ways to acknowledge and celebrate individual and team accomplishments, and most people management solutions offer such features. That being said, these tools might feel impersonal to some people, so don't overuse them.

Help Your Team Navigate Tough Times

One of the most important traits of a leadership position is resilience, the ability to recover from setbacks and face challenging circumstances. You might have experienced tight deadlines, unexpected technical issues, or organizational changes, but someone on your team may not. Don't assume everyone has thick skin—they need your guidance and support.

Once, I had to deal with a terrible security incident in which the company's code was leaked as part of the infamous Codecov supply chain breach. Attackers accessed hundreds of GitHub organizations, including ours, through a vulnerability in one of Codecov's scripts used to upload code coverage reports.

We had to work overtime and weekends for over a month to rotate access credentials and ensure no user data was leaked. If a database password was committed to the code by mistake, the attackers could find it, log in, and retrieve sensitive user data. It was a race against time and, of course, extremely stressful.

There was confusion, frustration, and fear during the first couple of days of the incident. Some people rushed into action and started changing passwords, but we weren't sure whether the attackers still had access to our GitHub organization, so changing passwords was futile. Before taking any further action, we needed to regain control.

After two months, the situation was resolved entirely without additional damage or loss of user data. The company made the incident public, apologized to our users, and took proper measures to prevent similar incidents from happening again.

Although I have faced many difficult times before, this experience taught me how to conduct myself and help my team navigate extreme situations. There are four things to do, in my opinion.

Remain Calm

The most important thing is to remain calm and focused, becoming the steadfast rock your team can rely on. If you lose your composure—by panicking, becoming angry, or becoming paralyzed by fear—your team will lose trust in your ability to lead. Maintaining your poise under pressure is crucial for inspiring a sense of confidence.

Reacting without thinking and making rushed decisions can make things worse, much worse. If you feel yourself losing control of your emotions, take a few moments to calm down and assess the next steps.

Acknowledge the Challenge

Pretending that everything is fine is counterproductive. Everyone is aware—or at least suspects—that problems exist, and trying to ignore or hide them only increases anxiety. You are responsible for remaining honest and acknowledging issues promptly and openly, even if you don't have a solution yet. Let your team know that you are prepared to take action and address the challenges together.

Get your team into the same room and explain exactly what the problem is. Let them know that hard times are ahead and that you'll need everyone's commitment to resolve it.

Come Up with a Plan

Gather your team to assess the situation, discuss potential solutions, and develop a clear and actionable plan. Craft a plan that clarifies who is responsible for each task and sets aggressive but realistic deadlines. This ensures that everyone understands their responsibility to address the issue.

As part of your plan, establish clear exit criteria. How will you know when the critical situation is resolved? Define a specific, measurable goal to achieve. In emergencies, goals are often straightforward—such as restoring website functionality or resolving a showstopper bug.

If the severity of the situation warrants it, communicate the plan to the broader organization to maintain transparency. Sharing this information openly helps build trust, aligns everyone, and guarantees that all stakeholders are informed about the steps to resolve the issue.

Celebrate Small Victories

Recognize and celebrate small victories to reinforce a sense of progress and keep the team motivated. This positive reinforcement helps maintain momentum and encourages them to stay committed despite the difficulties.

We humans need encouragement to keep going. Celebrations can take many forms, ranging from a quick shoutout in a team chat to a personalized thank-you message or acknowledging someone's effort during a meeting.

Small wins deserve immediate acknowledgment, but big celebrations should be reserved when the situation is resolved, or a significant milestone is achieved. These larger celebrations can be more elaborate, such as team lunches, award ceremonies, or public recognition at a company-wide event.

Key Points

- Balancing organizational goals and team needs requires empathy and diplomacy, but prioritizing the team often yields long-term benefits.

- Advocate for flexibility in work policies, such as remote work and autonomy in project selection, to improve team satisfaction.

- Equip your team with high-quality hardware, software tools, and learning resources to enhance productivity and innovation.

- Publicly acknowledge achievements to boost morale, reinforce contributions, and create a culture of appreciation.

- Remain calm and composed during crises, acknowledge challenges openly, and create actionable plans to address issues.

CHAPTER 3

Acquire Talent

Talent acquisition is one of the most important of your responsibilities. Identify, attract, and hire engineers who have the skills and experience, as well as a good culture fit and resonate with your mission.

In the popular book *Good to Great: Why Some Companies Make the Leap...And Others Don't*, Jim Collins expresses the importance of hiring the right people: "First Who ... Then What. We expected that good-to-great leaders would begin by setting a new vision and strategy. We found instead that they first got the right people on the bus, the wrong people off the bus, and the right people in the right seats—and then they figured out where to drive it."

First, who, then what.

Cultural fit goes beyond shared interests; it encompasses values, work ethics, and communication styles. Candidates who align with your organization's culture will likely commit and thrive. Those who resonate with your mission bring passion and intrinsic motivation to their work. They understand the bigger picture and are driven to contribute regardless of their official role.

Your job is to identify, attract, and hire these individuals.

Factors outside your control, such as the state of the economy, the job market, and your organization's reputation, can make this challenging. Economic fluctuations can impact budget allocations, while a competitive job market may affect your ability to attract talent. Additionally, your organization's reputation plays a role in influencing candidate perceptions.

© Jonathan Sosa 2025
J. Sosa, *From Culture to Code*, Apress Pocket Guides,
https://doi.org/10.1007/979-8-8688-1428-0_3

Write Effective Job Descriptions

Before attempting to hire, take the time to clarify what you're hiring for. Define what the ideal engineer for this position looks like. What skills, experience, and abilities do they possess? What is it about them that makes them successful? You can ask your team for feedback on what kind of person they want to work with.

It is also helpful to define the nonnegotiables upfront, which are the critical requirements someone in this position must meet. For example, experience working with server APIs could be a nonnegotiable requirement for a back-end engineer position.

A well-crafted job description is more than just a list of duties and requirements; it is your organization's first impression of potential candidates. It is a marketing tool that conveys the position's attractiveness and your organization's unique opportunities to attract top talent.

An effective job description should contain five main sections: an introduction, expectations, required skills and qualifications, nice-to-haves, and additional information about the position. If your organization has a predefined format for job descriptions and misses any of this information, I suggest you add it.

Introduction of the Organization, the Team, and Why You Are Hiring

Start by providing a compelling overview of your organization. Highlight the mission, values, culture, and achievements that set you apart in the industry. Showcase what makes your organization a great workplace.

Introduce the specific team or department, mentioning their goals, projects, and how they contribute to the organization's success. Explain the reason behind the job opening—whether due to organization growth, a new project, or replacing a departing team member. This context helps candidates understand the importance of the role and generates excitement about the opportunity.

Expectations Toward This Position

Clearly outline what the role entails by detailing the primary responsibilities and day-to-day tasks. Describe the objectives the candidate is expected to achieve and how their contributions will impact the team and the organization. Be specific about the scope of the role, including any leadership responsibilities, cross-functional collaboration, or unique challenges. Providing a transparent view of the position helps candidates assess their fit. It prepares them for what to expect.

Required Skills and Qualifications

List the essential qualifications and skills necessary for the role. They may include educational background, years of experience in specific fields, technical proficiencies, certifications, or soft skills like communication and problem-solving abilities. Be precise to ensure that applicants understand what is nonnegotiable. This section acts as a filter to attract candidates who meet the fundamental requirements.

Be mindful not to demand too much, as it can significantly narrow your pool of candidates. I've come across job descriptions that request five years of experience for a junior position, which is unrealistic. You have to be reasonable. Additionally, double-check that the technologies you require have been around long enough. Nothing can be more deterrent to a potential candidate than a generic or unrealistic job description.

Nice-to-Haves

In addition to the required qualifications, identify additional skills, experiences, or attributes that would be valuable, though not strictly required. These "nice-to-haves" might include familiarity with specialized software tools, previous experience in a related industry, multilingual abilities, or knowledge of particular methodologies and frameworks.

These could be familiarity with specific software, experience in a related industry, multilingual abilities, or knowledge of specific methodologies. Including these supplemental qualities allows you to recognize candidates who bring extra value to the role.

I've had candidates with a combination of several "nice-to-have" skills that compensated for the absence of one required qualification. For example, once, we hired a back-end engineer who didn't have the necessary experience with Google Cloud Platform but worked extensively with AWS and Azure, and they were familiar with our business domain.

Additional Information

Work hours, location, benefits, and any information about compensation that you can share. Make sure to showcase any perks that set your organization apart, such as flexible working hours, generous maternity and paternity leave policies, paid team lunches, the option to work remotely, the ability to choose your own computer, and an educational budget for professional development. Providing candidates with transparency about the work environment and available support structures can make your organization significantly more appealing, as it conveys respect for their time, well-being, and long-term growth.

I've discovered that these kinds of perks and benefits are surprisingly important to candidates. While competitive compensation is still a key factor, many job seekers also prioritize aspects that contribute to a higher quality of life and job satisfaction.

Attract Potential Candidates

Identifying and attracting potential candidates is not solely the responsibility of the talent acquisition department; it is also an important part of your role as an engineering leader. If you develop a strong reputation in the tech community and are able to convey the attractiveness of your team and workplace, you can become a magnet for top talent wherever you go. The best want to work with the best.

I'm very thankful that some of the best engineers I've worked with follow me to new companies whenever I change jobs. This consistent support is a testament to the strong relationships and trust I've built over the years. And I'm confident I can quickly assemble a small team of capable engineers if I pursue a new venture. Similarly, I've also changed jobs to work with someone I admire. I believe this skill is particularly valuable for startups, which often need to build teams rapidly to hit the ground running.

Publish an Engineering Blog

Writing blog posts about your team's projects, challenges, and solutions demonstrates your commitment to innovation and technical excellence. It lets you highlight cutting-edge technologies, methodologies, and best practices your team employs. Potential candidates who read your blog can gain insights into your culture and values.

Contribute to Open Source Projects

By participating in open source initiatives, your team shows a willingness to contribute to the broader tech community. This openness can be attractive to developers who value collaboration and shared learning. Regular contributions can increase your organization's visibility among developers who use or contribute to the same projects.

Your engineers could contribute to projects that you're already consuming in your product, like a framework or a library. They can register their affiliation in their profiles or, even better, make your organization name part of their account name.

Speak at Events

Speaking at conferences, meetups, or webinars helps establish your presence in your field. This can attract potential candidates. These engagements create opportunities to connect with like-minded professionals who might be curious about your projects. Even if they are not looking to change jobs immediately, they could reach out later in their careers if you made a good impression.

The real value of these events isn't the content—it's the relationships you build. I can hardly recall what I talked about during my speaking engagements, but some of the connections I made with the people I met there continue to this day.

Sponsor

Sponsoring hackathons, coding boot camps, tech events, or tech nonprofits demonstrates your organization's commitment to fostering growth and education. Sponsors often receive benefits like speaking slots, booth space, or attendee lists, which you can leverage to grow your brand and benefit recruitment.

In most cases, the cost of sponsorship justifies the return. Although it might not pay off immediately, it will in the future. Consider it a long-term investment.

Set Up the Hiring Pipeline

To streamline the hiring process, explicitly define and document the pipeline for each open position, including the hiring manager and the interviewers, and what they will be assessing for at each step. This will help the talent acquisition team know who to send the candidates to in each interview step and who will be responsible for making the final hiring decision.

Before starting the process, hold a kickoff meeting with all involved in the pipeline: the hiring manager, interviewers, and talent acquisition representatives. The goal of this meeting is for everyone to understand the job opening, its responsibilities, its expected seniority level, and what interviewers should be assessing for. The types of questions you should ask a junior engineer are very different from those for a staff engineer.

Hiring is often a critical, high-priority initiative for organizations. Ensure that everyone involved in the hiring pipeline understands its significance and approaches it with the necessary focus and urgency. Since hiring pipelines are inherently linear, progress depends on timely feedback from each interviewer. Without clear and prompt input from earlier stages, advancing a candidate to the next step is impossible, causing delays in the process.

In general, I recommend five steps for a comprehensive assessment of the candidates: resume screening, technical screening, culture fit interview, hiring manager interview, and senior leadership interview, in that order. Some companies have a longer hiring process, but in my view, no matter how thorough the interview process is, there's only so much you can learn about a candidate. The real test comes when they join the team and demonstrate their abilities in real-world scenarios.

Resume Screening

The hiring manager reviews the resumes recruiters submit to identify promising candidates. This process involves assessing the craftsmanship of each resume and evaluating the relevance of the candidate's skills, experience, and education to the job requirements. The hiring manager looks for signs of career progression, notable achievements, experience, and potential cultural fit while remaining alert to any red flags.

The last time I had to screen resumes was for a senior back-end engineer position I published on LinkedIn. To my surprise, I received over a thousand applications. I was spending too much time every day looking at resumes, so I had to enable filters. You'll likely have to implement some automation to limit the number of resumes reaching you or your team.

Technical Screening

Collect evidence of the candidate's technical skills. This screening can be an interview with one of our engineers or a take-home assignment. Many online tools, like HackerRank and LeetCode, can partially automate this step, but remember that cheating is easy nowadays, so take the results with a grain of salt.

I've found that candidates dislike long take-home assignments. Nobody wants to spend their weekend doing unpaid work. If you decide to implement one, I suggest keeping it under two hours. Typically, I prefer to invest time and do the technical screening in real time during an interview. This approach makes it significantly harder for candidates to cheat, allowing the interviewer to steer the conversation to dive into details and get a more comprehensive assessment.

Whenever you choose a take-home assignment or a real-time test, it's important to keep it relevant to the challenges they face daily on the job. I prefer an engineer who can solve actual problems rather than someone who has memorized a sort algorithm.

Culture Fit Interview

Assess how well the candidate aligns with our organization's values, work environment, and team dynamics. This interview is typically conducted by long-tenured team members who deeply understand the company's culture and are skilled at identifying soft skills, communication styles, and adaptability. It often explores areas such as the candidate's work ethic, experiences collaborating with others, and their approach to handling conflict, feedback, and challenging situations.

This type of interview is particularly nuanced because it lacks a standardized scoring system and relies heavily on the interviewer's perception and judgment. To improve consistency, I recommend interviewers prepare a structured set of questions and focus on specific examples from the candidate's past experiences.

Hiring Manager Interview

The hiring manager conducts a comprehensive interview to delve deeper into the candidate's experience, qualifications, and suitability for the role. This is an opportunity to discuss specific responsibilities, expectations, and how the candidate's experience and skills align with the position's requirements.

The hiring manager can also address concerns from previous stages, so they must review the feedback from previous interviewers and identify areas where the candidate's responses may have been unclear.

Senior Leadership Interview

The VP of Engineering, CTO, or equivalent senior-level position interviews the candidate. At this point, the team is confident in moving forward, so the interviewer should spend most of the time conveying the organization's appeal, selling the position, and answering the candidate's questions. There is no need to investigate the candidate's technical skills further, as they have been verified in previous interviews.

Due to my senior roles, this is the type of interview I've conducted most frequently over the past few years. During these interviews, I like to be open and give the candidate insight into what my team and I are working on and the problems we're facing. I'm very deliberate about what I talk about. I assess two things: how closely the candidate can follow the conversation and if they can give me suggestions about potential solutions.

I also pay a lot of attention to the candidate's questions. First of all, if they are genuinely enthusiastic about the opportunity, they will have questions. If not, it's a red flag, in my view. The questions I appreciate most from candidates are those about my team, the organization's culture, and upcoming projects. These inquiries show me that the candidate is thoughtfully evaluating whether we would be a good fit and considering what their career might look like if they took the opportunity.

Interview and Assess

An interview should be a two-way conversation that allows both the interviewer and the candidate to assess compatibility and fit. It's not just about evaluating the candidate's qualifications, experience, and skillset; it's also a critical chance for the candidate to ask thoughtful questions about the role, the team, and the organization's culture.

You should reserve enough time for interviews. I recommend at least one hour. This timeframe gives enough room to delve into the candidate's past experiences, explore their skills, and address any questions or concerns they may have.

Each interviewer may have their particular style and questions to ask. I make sure to seek the following:

- Evidence of past leadership

- Evidence of ability to learn quickly while on the job

- Evidence of understanding of the technologies required

- Clear and concise communication

- Interest in the team, organization, or industry

Conversely, these are the things I always avoid in interviews:

- Questions that an Internet search could quickly answer

- Trivia or tricky questions

- Questions about personal preferences, politics, or religion

Before sending the candidate to the last interview with senior leadership, I suggest the interviewers gather for a comprehensive discussion. This meeting allows each interviewer to share their perspectives, observations, and concerns. By pooling insights from different stages of the process, the hiring team gains a holistic understanding of the candidate's suitability for the role and the organization.

The goal is to reach a consensus on whether to hire the candidate. Achieving consensus is ideal because it reflects a collective agreement and confidence in the candidate's potential contribution to the team.

However, consensus is not a strict requirement. The hiring manager has the authority and responsibility to make the final decision. Even if the candidate did not perform exceptionally well in one of the interviews, the hiring manager might choose to proceed with an offer based on the overall assessment and the candidate's potential. The hiring manager might recognize qualities in the candidate that align strongly with the team's needs or the organization's strategic goals, which may outweigh shortcomings pointed out by other interviewers.

In fact, some of my best hires were initially rejected at various stages of the hiring process, but I chose to move forward anyway. One particular instance involved a candidate who struggled to answer a few questions during the technical interview, leading the interviewer to reject him.

However, I was impressed by the candidate's attention to detail demonstrated in his programming assignment. I took the time to explain my perspective to the interview panel and successfully convinced them to reconsider his application. This engineer went on to be promoted twice and remains a strong leader today. This experience reinforced the importance of looking beyond initial impressions and recognizing the potential that may not be immediately apparent to some during the interview process.

Hire Candidates

Once the decision to hire a candidate has been made, it's time to collaborate with the Human Resources department to draft an offer letter. They will need information about the candidate's seniority level, experience, and role to propose a compensation package.

Most organizations utilize a predefined salary range table to determine the initial offer based on these factors. A common practice is to offer around 80% of the maximum available budget for the position, leaving the remaining 20% as room for negotiation. It's up to the hiring manager to finalize the offer within this range, balancing budget constraints with the candidate's salary expectations.

When making an offer, think about the candidate's career path in the organization. I suggest you keep room for compensation growth within the position's range. In other words, avoid offering the maximum amount for the position right off the bat.

Once the offer is finalized, the most effective way to deliver it is in person. Inviting the candidate to a lunch meeting with the hiring manager and potential team members is an excellent approach. This setting allows the candidate to ask additional questions and become acquainted with the people they would be working alongside. It also provides an opportunity to generate excitement about current and future projects, giving the candidate a glimpse into the team's dynamics and the organization's vision.

After lunch, you can present the offer letter to the candidate. Delivering the offer in person adds a personal touch and reinforces your interest in the candidate. It also allows for immediate discussion of any questions or concerns the candidate may have regarding the offer, benefits, or next steps.

Some candidates will accept the offer immediately, and others will ask for time to think. Have Human Resources write a deadline on the offer; I recommend one week. It's enough time to think and consult with their family. While you await their decision, you may need to put other candidates on hold, risking losing them, so be firm with the deadline. Don't wait too long for their response.

There will be candidates who interview with multiple companies simultaneously. More power to them; I've done this myself. Just be careful not to engage in a bidding war. Remember, it's not just about money—you want people who are genuinely interested in working with you. If they decide to accept a different offer, so be it. Move on and continue looking.

Onboard New Hires

New hires should begin contributing to the team as soon as possible. While the hire's level and skill set are also factors, the quality and completeness of the onboarding process play a role in determining how quickly they can start adding value. The key to a successful onboarding is to be supportive and not assume anything. Things that might appear obvious to you may be entirely unknown for new hires.

The first thing is to get the basics right. Verify your IT department has a process for purchasing and configuring a computer, setting up an email address, and providing access to all the organization's internal tools. All this has to be ready by day one. Many computer manufacturers offer business programs that provide preconfigured computers with software installed out of the box. If your organization doesn't use one already, I suggest you look into them.

Invest in building well-structured and comprehensive onboarding documentation and a process that can help new team members familiarize themselves with the policies, tools, workflows, goals, and expectations. Request a product or sales representative to introduce the software from a nontechnical, end-user perspective.

Following are the pieces I recommend you have ready for them.

Team Onboarding Documentation

Provide a detailed overview of the team structure, including each member's roles and responsibilities, to help the new hire understand whom to approach for specific questions.

Summarize current and upcoming projects, their objectives, timelines, and how they align with broader goals.

Likely already covered by employee onboarding, add links to organization policies, communication protocols, development processes, and compliance requirements.

All documentation should stay up to date and evolve along the organization and team.

Repository README

The README file in the code repository should offer comprehensive, step-by-step instructions for configuring the local development environment from start to finish. This includes prerequisites like hardware requirements, software installations, environment variables, and specific configurations.

The README should also include links to the coding conventions, formatting standards, and best practices the team follows. It should also anticipate common issues that might arise during setup and provide solutions under a troubleshooting section. Save the new hire from wasting time investigating a problem someone else has already resolved.

I suggest crafting a Code of Conduct as part of the README. A Code of Conduct is a set of guidelines and standards that outline the expected behavior and interactions within the repository's contributors. Its main components are expected behavior, unacceptable behavior and its consequences, and reporting mechanisms.

Have new hires update the README as they go through it for the first time. As software evolves, the development environment must adapt to it. They might encounter a setup step that is no longer needed or, conversely, a dependency requiring additional configuration. This resource is a living document that is never finished.

Mentor Support

Pair the new hire with an experienced team member who can be their go-to person for questions, guidance, and support during onboarding, typically for the first month. This relationship is mutually beneficial: the new hire receives the support they need to ramp up, while the team member has the opportunity to practice formal mentorship—a fundamental skill for senior engineers. Mentorship plays a pivotal role in the growth of individuals and teams, yet it often goes unnoticed in formal performance reviews. Make sure to acknowledge and celebrate it.

Work with the mentor to establish clear, achievable goals for the onboarding period, ensuring they align with the new hire's role and the team's objectives. These goals should provide a structured path for the new hire to gradually build confidence and familiarity with the code base and the team's workflows, tools, and culture. Early milestones like fixing a bug, implementing a minor feature, or drafting a technical document are good ways to encourage hands-on learning. The sooner you start seeing tangible contributions, the better. Celebrate them publicly to give a sense of accomplishment to the new hire.

Bring in External Help When Necessary

In all the companies I've worked for, we've had consultants at some point. I've found that temporarily bringing external help to strengthen a team is very common in software development. It's typically quicker to find someone than a full-time employee, as agencies have talent pools to pick from—you just need to let them know the skill set you're looking for, and they'll find a match for you.

If you compare the cost-per-hour between a full-time employee and a consultant of similar seniority and skill set, the consultant is almost always higher. This is because you have to pay a premium for the convenience of timeboxing the engagement. You don't need to worry about benefits, labor laws, or other implications of bringing someone into your payroll.

In general, I recommend a minimum engagement of three months for any external consultant. They need time to ramp up, familiarize themselves with the software, and integrate with the team. A couple of weeks will likely pass before they're ready to make meaningful contributions.

External help should be a last resort, but there are two key scenarios where it makes sense to bring it in:

- When you cannot extend the deadline or reduce the product scope, and your team is overwhelmed

- When a project requires niche knowledge or skills that aren't available in-house

The biggest downside of relying heavily on consultants is that they'll leave and take the experience with them. Have them thoroughly document their efforts and mentor your core team to guarantee that someone can continue their work after they're gone.

Key Points

- Focus on identifying candidates who align with the organization's values, work ethics, and mission.

- A job description should act as both a filter and a marketing tool, clearly outlining expectations, required qualifications, and "nice-to-haves."

- Define and streamline a multistep hiring process, including resume screening, technical assessments, cultural fit evaluation, and leadership interviews.

- Engage with mediums like blogs, open source projects, tech events, and sponsorships to reach diverse audiences and build a talent pipeline.

- Provide clear onboarding documentation, comprehensive READMEs, and structured mentoring to help new hires ramp up quickly and feel supported.

CHAPTER 4

Organize Your People

Any large software development effort requires a lot of engineers—and whenever you have a lot of engineers or a few, you have to figure out how to divide them into effective teams based on factors like the nature of the software you develop, the available talent, and the organization's objectives.

It is well known that some attributes of high-performing teams are clear goals, diverse skill sets, strong cohesion, and mutual trust among members. However, an often overlooked element is the effectiveness of team interfaces—how well people communicate and collaborate. Poor team interfaces can lead to fragmented communication, duplicated efforts, and misaligned priorities. In simpler words, you have to be concerned not only about how well a team works as a unit but also how well it works with other teams.

The two traditional, simplest ways of grouping people into development teams are by function and by project. If you're part of a small organization like a startup, one of these two types should suffice. Let's explore their pros and cons.

Form Teams by Function or by Project

A function is an area of responsibility, usually involving specialized technology or platforms. Some typical functions in software engineering organizations are back end, front end, data, server infrastructure, and, more recently, machine learning.

© Jonathan Sosa 2025
J. Sosa, *From Culture to Code*, Apress Pocket Guides,
https://doi.org/10.1007/979-8-8688-1428-0_4

Regardless of their functions, individuals work together on specific projects toward a common objective. In software development, a project is a set of activities in the development process for a particular product or service.

Function-alignment strengths	Project-alignment strengths
A stable structure allows for long-term planning and team cohesion. Clear paths for technical skill advancement. A high degree of expertise within a specific function. Shared language and understanding among specialists. Consistent standards and practices within a function. Easier to implement technical best practices.	Team members gain diverse experience. Encourages versatility and adaptability among team members. Efficient project execution with dedicated resources. Minimizes delays from cross-functional coordination. Faster decision-making for projects. All key stakeholders are within the team. Clear accountability for project outcomes. A more holistic view of project challenges and risks.

If the product road map is well defined and your team has the experience to deliver it, I recommend adopting function-aligned reporting lines. This structure allows work to be streamlined more efficiently by grouping team members based on their specialization.

Conversely, adopting project-aligned reporting lines may be more beneficial if there are many unknowns and a need for discovery and iteration. This approach enables different disciplines within the team to collaborate more cohesively on specific projects. For example, a startup striving to reach product-market fit might benefit from a project-aligned structure, as it facilitates flexibility, rapid iteration, and close collaboration among different disciplines.

In my career, I've seen functional teams deliver results quickly in the early stages of a project but eventually become siloed, leading to reduced collaboration and communication with other teams.

Ultimately, the decision depends on your specific circumstances. Whichever approach you choose doesn't have to be permanent; you can always pivot based on how well it works for you. Keep your ears open for feedback.

Consider the Team Topologies Framework

There are more elaborate ways to organize teams, which might be more effective for larger organizations. I'm personally a fan of the Team Topologies framework created by Matthew Skelton and Manuel Pais. Team Topologies is a modern approach to structuring and organizing teams that optimizes collaboration, information flow, and delivery in complex software systems.

This framework emphasizes four fundamental team types: stream-aligned teams, platform teams, complicated subsystem teams, and enabling teams—each with distinct responsibilities. The framework's main objectives are to reduce each member's cognitive load and improve interactions between individuals and teams.

While only larger organizations require all four types of teams, a common mistake is having all engineers solely focused on product features. Without dedicated teams to support foundational aspects like infrastructure, tooling, and complicated subsystems, the delivery of value slows down over time.

I'll give you the basics of these team types, but I encourage you to study the book *Team Topologies: Organizing Business and Technology Teams for Fast Flow* for a more in-depth understanding.

Stream-Aligned Teams

These are aligned to a specific business domain or product/service flow. They own the end-to-end delivery of a product or service and are responsible for directly delivering value to the customer. They are outcome-oriented.

Each stream-aligned team is full-stack and full-lifecycle. It's responsible for front end, back end, UX design, testing, deployment, and monitoring.

Enabling Teams

Their primary function is to help other teams adopt and improve their practices, capabilities, and processes. They often work with stream-aligned teams to assist in areas needing more in-depth expertise.

For example, a security specialist belonging to an enabling team may spend more time studying security issues than would be possible as a member of a stream-aligned team.

Complicated Subsystem Teams

These teams focus on areas of the system that require specialist knowledge with a longer focus. They handle complex subsystems that other teams can't deal with due to specialized knowledge requirements.

For example, if you offer a streaming service, you might have a video encoding team focusing solely on algorithms to improve video quality.

Platform Teams

Platform teams aim to provide internal services, tools, and frameworks to reduce cognitive load. They maintain common infrastructure and services and keep them reliable and easy for other teams to use.

Infrastructure-as-a-Service (IaaS) teams are one example of a typical platform team. They manage infrastructure and self-service dashboards for stream-aligned teams to spin up resources.

Reduce Cognitive Load and Cross-Team Interactions

To reduce cognitive load as part of a team, focus on limiting the amount of information and complexity each team member must handle. Clearly defining roles and responsibilities allows individuals to concentrate on specific areas without being overwhelmed by unrelated tasks.

Similarly, to reduce cross-team interactions, design teams to be as autonomous as possible by clearly defining their boundaries and responsibilities. This involves aligning teams around specific services or product areas—allowing them to operate independently without requiring frequent coordination with others.

You should implement standardized interfaces and communication protocols to minimize the necessity for direct interactions between teams. These standards serve as a common language, ensuring teams can work independently while maintaining alignment and avoiding bottlenecks. For example, if the front-end team requires a new back-end API method, they can create a mock version themselves using a predefined template without waiting for the back-end team to implement it.

Choose the Right Engineering Managers

Changing an engineer's role from individual contributor (IC) to manager is a significant career shift that involves more than just a title change. First, I suggest never considering a managerial role for someone with less than five years of successful experience as an IC—they need to have a deep, hands-on understanding of technology; otherwise, they won't be respected by their new direct reports.

That being said, it's a common mistake for organizations to transition a senior IC to a manager solely based on their strong technical skills. While technical expertise is valuable, managerial responsibilities require different competencies beyond individual performance.

As an IC, performance is mostly evaluated by their personal impact. In contrast, a manager's success is gauged by the team's overall impact. This shift from individual achievement to team success requires a change in mindset.

Converting technically skilled ICs to management roles can often mean stepping away from the hands-on work they excel at and enjoy. Ensure these engineers are willing and prepared to transition. They must fully understand the responsibilities and challenges of a managerial position, recognizing that their role will shift from executing tasks to overseeing and supporting their team. Observe their interactions with other engineers. They don't necessarily have to be your superstar engineer. In fact, sometimes, the superstar can deliver more value to the organization as an IC than as a manager.

I once saw a staff engineer being converted to an engineering manager almost against their will. It was evident that it was not the career path they wanted to take, but because of their expertise and longevity in the company, management pushed him to take on the role. Problems ensued: the new manager wasn't paying enough attention to their engineers, didn't listen to feedback, and instead used their newly acquired authority to push his initiatives forward. To everyone's relief, they were promptly converted back to IC after a few months.

Once you've decided to transition someone from an IC to a managerial position, you should make it as smooth as possible. A seamless transition benefits not only the individual stepping into the new role but also their new direct reports. Consider implementing a mentoring program where new managers can observe and learn from experienced ones. Regular check-ins between the new manager and their mentor can help address challenges early and make sure they feel supported in their new responsibilities. Additionally, your organization should provide structured training sessions focused on essential managerial skills. Hopefully, policies already exist to support this.

Finally, note that I don't use the word "promote" when describing the transition from IC to manager. I'm a strong proponent of having IC and management career paths run in parallel. Managers are not "above" ICs; they just have a different set of responsibilities. I've worked in companies with ICs who had an impact equivalent to that of a Director of Engineering, and they were compensated accordingly.

Key Points

- Organize teams by function for stability and expertise or by project for adaptability and rapid execution.

- Adopt the Team Topologies framework to optimize collaboration and reduce cognitive load in larger organizations.

- Clearly define roles and responsibilities within teams to limit the complexity individuals handle.

- Transitioning ICs to management roles requires careful consideration of their technical expertise, willingness, and ability to prioritize team success over individual contributions.

- High-performing teams need not only internal cohesion but also effective interfaces with other teams to avoid fragmentation and duplication.

CHAPTER 5

Set Expectations and Evaluate Against Them

When expectations are explicitly defined upfront, they create a shared understanding of standards and success criteria among everyone in the organization. Engineers benefit from knowing what is expected of them, as it provides a framework for prioritizing their efforts and measuring their progress. Moreover, well-defined expectations enable evaluations to be fair and constructive, as they are based on agreed-upon guidelines rather than subjective judgment.

Evaluations are important for engineers because they recognize their professional growth and contributions. They can also offer structured feedback, helping them understand how their performance is perceived, identify areas for improvement, and realign their efforts with broader goals.

For many, the term "evaluation" has a slightly negative connotation, likely stemming from experiences in school where it was synonymous with being graded or having mistakes pointed out in homework. Those moments could feel discouraging, as they often focus on what went wrong. However, in the professional world, I think feedback—when delivered correctly—that comes hand in hand with evaluations is a gift. Evaluations

© Jonathan Sosa 2025
J. Sosa, *From Culture to Code*, Apress Pocket Guides,
https://doi.org/10.1007/979-8-8688-1428-0_5

provide a unique opportunity to gain insights into how others perceive your work, uncover blind spots, and identify areas for improvement. Rather than being a punitive measure, they serve as a road map to growth. You should make this a part of your team culture.

That being said, you don't need to wait for the formal evaluation cycle to share feedback. The best time to give positive or negative feedback is in the moment. Sharing your real-time reaction to the engineer's behavior or results allows you to appreciate or correct them.

Define an Engineering Ladder

Different companies have different naming conventions and levels in their ladders. For example, Apple's ladder begins at ICT2 and goes up to ICT6. Netflix's ladder starts at L3 and goes up to L7. You can check out the website `https://www.levels.fyi` to see comparisons.

While having more levels in the ladder makes it more challenging to define and maintain, it gives engineers a stronger sense of progression as they can advance more frequently. For most companies, a five-level ladder seems to be the sweet spot.

Expectations can be commonly applied to all engineers or tailored to each engineering specialization. For example, a general expectation for a senior engineer, regardless of their specialization, might be, "Can deliver their code to the end user." In contrast, specialized expectations are tailored to the engineer's focus area. For instance, a senior back-end engineer should be able to "Deploy microservices to the cloud," while a senior iOS engineer should be capable of "Publishing an app to the App Store."

I've found that general expectations work best for most organizations for two main reasons:

- Engineers are less restricted to their area of expertise. Those contributing to multiple technologies and business domains can take the next most important task without depending on others. This fosters a versatile and impactful engineering team.

- Formulating, promoting, and maintaining specialized expectations can be overwhelming. For example, if your organization has five types of engineers, each with six levels, you would need 30 different sets of expectations. This effort could take you months.

The downside of general expectations is their inherent ambiguity, which can lead to misunderstandings and inconsistencies in performance standards. Some engineers might struggle to understand precisely what is expected of them, so managers need to provide additional clarity and offer tailored feedback during one-on-ones and goal-setting sessions.

Depending on the size of your organization and the desired level of granularity, defining engineer levels might take anywhere from a few weeks to several months. During this time, input from various teams will be gathered, and the definitions will be iterated to achieve a comprehensive and agreed-upon initial version. Reaching consensus is critical, as these levels will be applied to all engineers. Additionally, Human Resources must review and approve the defined engineer levels to align them appropriately with compensation structures.

Below is a basic engineering ladder to serve as a starting point for customization to your organization's needs.

Junior Engineer

- Less than two years of experience.

- They work under the supervision of more senior engineers and understand basic design patterns and their usefulness.

- They can formulate precise and concrete questions during coaching, work well in a team, constructively accept feedback, and communicate transparently.

- With a good grasp of the technologies, they can contribute new functionality with some assistance.

- They clearly understand what is expected of them and proactively consult their manager or team lead when unable to resolve a problem.

Intermediate Engineer

- Between two and five years of experience.

- They work effectively within a team, actively participate in meetings, provide reliable estimates, and identify and raise risks early.

- They contribute meaningfully to design and definition discussions and possess a strong understanding of core programming languages, their features, and the technologies used within the team.

- They can recognize and apply various design and architecture patterns, assisting others in identifying patterns or refactoring code.

- They conduct code reviews in their areas of expertise, deeply understand most of the code base, and contribute new functionality with little help.

Senior Engineer

- Between five and eight years of experience.

- They take leadership roles in projects, working closely with product managers to ensure user stories are well-defined, adequately estimated, and have clear acceptance criteria.

- As experts in one or more programming languages and technologies, they keep their skills up to date.

- With a deep understanding of design and architecture patterns, they can recommend their use in design documents and assist others.

- They actively seek opportunities to provide technical coaching and offer leadership when team members need encouragement, advice, support, or guidance.

Staff Engineer

- Between 8 and 12 years of experience.

- As an expert in multiple programming languages and technologies, they can solve high-pressure problems and advocate for properly using design patterns.

- They are patient and effective teachers for whom others actively seek guidance. They are capable of clearly communicating complex concepts to audiences with varying technical expertise.

- They write documentation to define best practices and protocols across the engineering organization.

- They provide strong leadership to overcome significant differences of opinion, negotiate and persuade effectively, and avoid dictating unless necessary.

Principal Engineer

- More than 12 years of experience.

- They serve as technical visionaries and leaders within the organization, driving the strategic direction of engineering efforts.

- They can solve the most complex and high-pressure technical challenges as experts in multiple programming languages and technologies.

- They are leaders who advocate adopting best practices in architecture and development practices across the organization.

- Their expertise extends beyond the organization through active participation in industry events, publications, and contributions to open source projects, establishing them as recognized figures in the tech community.

Again, these are merely guidelines—particularly talented engineers may not require five years to reach a senior level. It's important to recognize that career progression can vary significantly based on an individual's skills, experience, and contributions.

Expect the level definitions to evolve as engineers provide feedback, technology advances, and the organization's needs change. Actively seek input from your team to ensure the levels accurately reflect the current skills and responsibilities required for the role.

Decide the Frequency of Evaluations

In my experience, holding evaluations and promotions twice a year is the right balance between providing timely feedback and maintaining a sustainable workload for management and Human Resources.

When evaluations occur less frequently than twice a year—such as annually—the gap between opportunities becomes too large. If engineers expect a salary increase or promotion and miss it for any reason, they are faced with waiting an entire year for the next opportunity. This prolonged delay can be highly demotivating. The engineer may feel undervalued or overlooked, decreasing morale and productivity.

Conversely, I've worked in companies that held evaluations every quarter. While quarterly evaluations aim to provide frequent feedback and quick progression, in practice, they became an overwhelming amount of work for both management and Human Resources. Preparing for evaluations—gathering performance data, writing assessments, and conducting review meetings—requires significant time and effort. When repeated every three months, this process can consume a substantial portion of managers' time that they could otherwise spend on initiatives or supporting their teams in other ways.

Moreover, I saw some managers take shortcuts, resulting in unfair evaluations or insufficient feedback. The pressure to complete assessments quickly can compromise their quality and thoroughness. The constant cycle of evaluations can cause feedback fatigue, where both managers and engineers become desensitized to the process, diminishing its effectiveness.

Prepare Evaluations

Managers are responsible for systematically collecting evidence and feedback from various stakeholders to assess their engineers' performance. This process involves gathering quantitative data, such as task completion rates, code quality metrics, and qualitative feedback from peers and cross-functional teams.

Every engineer should be assessed using the same expectations, performance metrics, and standards, regardless of their specific team or department. Any form of bias or favoritism, even if unconscious, is unacceptable. I recommend conducting calibration meetings to ensure consistency and fairness in evaluations.

A calibration meeting is a structured session in which managers and Human Resources representatives review, discuss, and compare engineers' performance. The primary goal of this meeting is to ensure consistency, fairness, and objectivity in performance evaluations.

In a calibration meeting, managers present their comments about engineers' performance to the rest of the attendants and propose an evaluation grade. People in the room have the opportunity to offer additional feedback and agree or disagree with the grade. These discussions are expected to take time, so I suggest reserving at least fifteen minutes per engineer.

Some managers are "nicer" than others: they tend to give away higher performance ratings and even grant premature promotions to their team members. While their intentions might be to boost morale or reward their staff, this practice can cause significant organizational issues. It creates an unfair environment where employees from other teams, who may be performing at the same or even higher levels, do not receive equivalent recognition or advancement opportunities. This disparity can breed resentment, lower morale, and undermine trust in the organization's evaluation and promotion processes.

On the other hand, the opposite scenario can also occur: managers with excessively high standards or overly critical tendencies may fail to reward or promote deserving employees. This can result in talented employees feeling demotivated, undervalued, and overlooked, leading to increased frustration and turnover.

During calibration meetings, each engineer must be objectively assessed and compared to their peers across teams with similar seniority levels. This process ensures that performance ratings and promotions are based on merit, consistent criteria, and observable achievements rather than subjective judgments or managerial favoritism.

Deliver Evaluation Results

Deliver the evaluation results in person and privately. Choose a private and comfortable setting where the individual being evaluated feels safe and respected, minimizing any feelings of embarrassment or defensiveness. Approach the conversation with empathy and a genuine desire to support their growth.

Start by acknowledging the engineer's accomplishments and contributions, highlighting specific instances where they excelled. Then, transition into areas with room for growth by providing specific examples of behaviors or outcomes that need improvement. Avoid vague statements or try to guess the motivation behind the individual being evaluated. Instead, focus on observable concrete behaviors.

- "When you did this..."
- "When you said that..."
- "I would like you to change this behavior."
- "I would like you to complete this task."

Feedback should always be actionable and oriented toward future development. After discussing areas for improvement, work with the engineer to establish clear, achievable goals and provide the necessary resources or support to help them succeed. Whether it's additional training, mentorship, or adjusting workloads, show a commitment to their professional development. The core of delivering evaluation results lies in providing actionable feedback that the engineer can use to grow professionally. What was done is done.

When delivering a negative evaluation, avoid accusing and ask questions to elicit the other side's take on the issue instead. For example:

- I've heard we're behind schedule on your project. Is this accurate?
- We're seeing a rise in the number of bugs. What's your view on this problem?
- I get the impression that you're not as motivated as before. Can you help me understand why?
- I sense hostility between you and Mark. What's going on there?

The key is to open the conversation and welcome the individual's point of view. This communicates that you see them as a person and are aware of their vulnerability in the situation. You should aim to have a shared understanding of the issues.

Evaluation results should never surprise the engineer. Feedback should be given continually during regular interactions, one-on-ones, and meetings. By integrating consistent feedback into these frequent interactions, managers can address strengths and areas for improvement in real time, allowing engineers to make adjustments without waiting for the evaluations to come. If someone is shocked by an evaluation result, their manager didn't do their job properly.

Promote High Performers

When I first heard the term "10x engineer," referring to someone who performs ten times better than the average engineer, I thought it was an exaggeration. Surely, nobody could be that good, right? Well, it turns out it's not as far-fetched as I initially thought. According to the study *The Best and the Rest* by the Kelley School of Business, first published in 2021, high performers are generally 400% more productive than the average employee and as high as 800% more productive than average in complex occupations like software engineering.

Setting aside what "performance" really means for you, I'm sure there are engineers in your organization who push boundaries, inspire others, drive projects, and exceed expectations. Failing to identify and promote a deserving individual can lead to low morale and, eventually, loss of talent. On the other hand, promoting an undeserving engineer is demotivating to the rest of the team.

However, before considering an engineer for promotion, collect enough evidence to justify it to the organization. Personally, I need to see the engineer exceeding expectations for at least six months before I'm confident they are ready to perform consistently at the next level.

Prematurely promoting someone harms their career by giving them a false sense of growth. They might be happy with the increased compensation and the more prestigious job title, but they'll struggle to take on the added responsibilities.

It also damages the organization's trust in you as a leader and demotivates the rest of the team. Eventually, everyone will notice the mismatch between the new role's expectations and the individual's real competencies.

I recommend you prepare a recommendation letter outlining the reasons for the promotion for management to assess. This letter should contain four elements:

- The new level being proposed and why

- Evidence of a skill set matching the next level

- Evidence of successful project deliveries

- Testimonials supporting the promotion from at least two peers

Most organizations have a cap on the number of promotions they can grant each year, so there will likely be competition among managers on who gets them. A robust and well-crafted recommendation letter can be the deciding factor in securing a promotion for your engineer.

It is your responsibility to do your best to get them the recognition they deserve, but sometimes, budget limitations or financial constraints prevent promotions. If this is the case, keep the communication transparent and explain the situation to your engineer, emphasizing that their performance has been acknowledged and appreciated, even if the formal promotion cannot happen immediately.

Deal with Underperformers

Underperformers generally fall under one of two categories: those who are willing to work to improve and those who aren't. You can help the former, but not the latter. Don't waste time on people who have given up or are abusing the organization.

The first step is for you and the engineer to have an open, honest conversation to learn the cause or causes of underperforming. Of course, this conversation must be held privately and, ideally, in person. I advise you to spend most of the time asking questions and listening, but you must make it clear that expectations are not being met.

If you have high empathy, like me, you'll likely have difficulty with this type of conversation. The desire to avoid hurting someone's feelings can tempt you to soften your words. However, I urge you to be direct and clear. While it may feel uncomfortable at the moment, clarity is necessary for the individual to fully understand their situation and what's expected of them moving forward.

Sugarcoating the conversation can cause confusion, misinterpretation, and prolonged problems, ultimately doing more harm than good. Being empathetic doesn't mean avoiding difficult truths—it means delivering them with care and respect. You're not doing anyone a favor, on the contrary.

In my experience, the most common causes for underperforming are the following.

Lack of Understanding of Expectations

This is entirely management's fault. The individual simply doesn't understand what's expected of them, so they don't focus on the right things. The good news is that this problem is relatively easy to correct; you just need to show them the way. As I explained in previous chapters, setting proper goals and expectations is one of your primary responsibilities. If you encounter these underperformers often, it means you and the rest of the leadership team haven't put in enough effort in this area.

You can expect almost immediate performance improvements after you communicate the expectations.

Lack of Skills

Correcting this is also straightforward, but the engineer in question will need time to catch up, perhaps weeks or months. If the gap is significant, you should consider a temporary demotion or a transfer to a different team.

This situation suggests that a mistake may have occurred during the hiring process. For some reason, the engineer was placed at a level that exceeds their current competencies. This could stem from factors such as overestimating their skills during the interview process, inadequate assessment of their experience, or perhaps misaligned expectations between the candidate and the organization.

I suggest you assign a mentor, someone with experience and patience, to guide the challenged engineer and help them catch up. If you see potential and have a good attitude, you can also invest in formal training, online courses, and books to accelerate the process.

Personal Issues

Personal issues are generally out of your control. A breakup; a sick child; an illness, either physical or mental; or an aging parent could be legitimate reasons an engineer couldn't focus on work. The manager should have a sense that something like this is happening based on one-on-one conversations.

Experienced managers will notice problems before they start affecting the engineer's performance. Some signs are being late to or missing meetings, lack of participation, falling behind on code assignments, and constant distraction.

If your organization permits, consider offering flexible working hours or the option to work remotely better to support the individual's needs during a difficult time. For more severe issues, explore the possibility of a leave of absence to allow ample time and space to focus on resolving their challenges fully without the added pressure of work responsibilities. Showing the proper care and understanding during difficult times can often translate to retaining talent for a long time.

Lack of Desire to Contribute

The individual has become disengaged and appears to lack the motivation to contribute meaningfully to their role. This behavior often signifies a deeper issue: they may have mentally checked out of their responsibilities and are merely going through the motions, showing up for work without the intention of improving their performance.

In my experience, the situation is rarely salvageable when someone reaches this point. Attempts to reengage them are often met with resistance or apathy, as they may have already consciously or unconsciously decided that their future does not align with the organization's path. Continuing to accommodate such behavior can set a dangerous precedent, implying that underperformance is acceptable.

Moreover, this situation can significantly harm team morale. Team members likely notice when someone is not meeting expectations or pulling their weight. This can breed resentment, particularly among high-performing individuals working hard and feeling burdened by the slack left behind. It can also undermine the credibility of leadership if the lack of accountability is perceived as tolerance for mediocrity.

Therefore, consider taking prompt action by initiating a Performance Improvement Plan (PIP) or even transitioning the individual out of the organization. Given the legal implications of such serious measures, consult with your organization's Human Resources or equivalent department on how to proceed.

As mentioned in previous chapters, it's critical to remain calm and measured in your words and actions. Addressing an individual with a persistently bad attitude can be both draining and frustrating, but losing your composure can escalate the situation or even undermine your position.

Key Points

- A well-structured career ladder provides engineers with a road map for growth, detailing expectations, responsibilities, and progression at each level.

- Evaluations provide structured feedback, helping engineers align with organizational goals and identify areas for growth.

- Conduct evaluations semiannually to provide timely feedback and opportunities for salary adjustments or promotions without overwhelming managers and HR.

- Use objective metrics, stakeholder input, and calibration meetings to ensure consistency and fairness across teams and avoid favoritism.

- Promote engineers who consistently exceed expectations for at least six months and provide evidence of their readiness.

CHAPTER 6

Set Goals

To be successful, everyone in the organization must be aligned and committed to working toward concrete goals. These goals are derived from a fundamental question: "What is most important to achieve?" By focusing on this priority, the organization can direct its efforts toward what truly matters, ensuring that every initiative and task contributes to a vision.

Without goals, employees often experience a lack of motivation and purpose, as they may not understand how their work contributes to the bigger picture. This can lead to reduced engagement and morale, as people tend to be less inspired when they don't see clear outcomes tied to their efforts. Decision-making becomes increasingly challenging, with leaders lacking a framework to evaluate initiatives or measure progress. Ultimately, an organization without goals is likely to struggle with growth.

The Objective, Key Results (OKRs) framework is my preferred method for defining goals. It was created by John Doerr, a famous venture capitalist who has worked with companies like Google, Intel, and the Gates Foundation. Simply put, OKRs help you say, "Here's our big goal, and here are the concrete ways we'll know we're getting there." They keep everyone focused on the same priority and make it easy to check in on progress.

For a deeper understanding of OKRs, I highly recommend reading John Doerr's excellent book *Measure What Matters*. In this section, I'll explain just the basics.

© Jonathan Sosa 2025
J. Sosa, *From Culture to Code*, Apress Pocket Guides,
https://doi.org/10.1007/979-8-8688-1428-0_6

Define Team OKRs

Define Objectives

Objectives are the what—they're the big, exciting goals you want to accomplish. Think of them as clear, inspiring statements that give you direction. For example: "Become the go-to app for healthy recipes." or "Double our team's development velocity."

When defining objectives, focus on creating clear, concise, and inspiring statements defining your aim. Objectives should be ambitious yet attainable, aligning with your organization's mission and strategy. They must be qualitative and action-oriented, providing a clear direction without detailing the steps. When crafting objectives, use motivational and easy-to-understand language, ensuring all team members can rally around them.

Your objectives need a time limit. While most organizations set their objectives every quarter, it is also okay to set longer-term objectives.

Define Key Results

Key results are the how—they're specific, measurable steps that show you've reached your objective. They act like signposts along the way. For instance: "Increase app downloads by 20%." and "Reduce project turnaround time by 15%."

They have to be challenging yet attainable, pushing the team to excel without setting unrealistic expectations. When crafting key results, keep them aligned with the objective. Use meaningful and relevant metrics, and avoid vanity metrics that do not contribute to the core goal.

Here are some examples of OKRs.

Objective: Enhance Website Performance and User Experience

- Key result 1: Decrease website load time from five seconds to under two seconds.

- Key result 2: Improve user retention rate from 40% to 60%.

- Key result 3: Increase conversion rate from 2% to 5%.

Objective: Improve Customer Satisfaction

- Key result 1: Increase the Net Promoter Score (NPS) from 45 to 60 by the end of Q2.

- Key result 2: Reduce average customer support response time from 24 to 4 hours within 3 months.

- Key result 3: Achieve a customer satisfaction rating of at least 90% in postservice surveys by year end.

Objective: Improve Product Quality and Reliability

- Key result 1: Reduce product defect rate from 5% to 1% within the next quarter.

- Key result 2: Decrease the number of P1 bugs reported by the QA team by 30%.

- Key result 3: Decrease customer-reported issues by 50% over the next six months.

You need to secure buy-in for your team's OKRs from two groups of stakeholders: your superiors and, of course, your team members. Involving them early in the drafting stage allows everyone to provide feedback and be part of the decision-making process.

Organize separate sessions for each group early in the drafting stage and present your draft OKRs. I prefer to have a session with my team first to allow them to raise concerns, share new ideas, and improve the draft before bringing it to my superiors.

Keep Track of Team OKRs

To track OKR progress, establish a regular review process that includes setting clear timelines and milestones for each objective and key result. I recommend biweekly check-in sessions with your team to share progress, address challenges, and make adjustments as necessary. Additionally, OKR conversations should be incorporated into the one-on-one meetings so that you can explore the details more deeply and support your engineers.

For transparency, document and make your team's OKRs and progress accessible to the whole organization. When someone asks about them, send them the link. There are plenty of dedicated OKR management tools out there. The project management tool you use today likely has an OKR management feature. If it doesn't, you can create a web page with a table containing OKRs, their owners, and current progress.

You can and should modify your OKRs if there are significant changes in priorities, organization goals, or external circumstances. OKRs are meant to be flexible and aligned with the current focus. However, you must communicate and document the reasons for the changes clearly and be prepared to address questions about the changes. Stakeholders will hold you accountable and may seek to confirm whether the adjustments result from adapting to evolving priorities or merely attempting to move the goalposts to buy more time. Transparency is key to maintaining trust and understanding among all team members and stakeholders.

Consider Introducing Personal OKRs

Unlike team OKRs, which focus on collective objectives, personal OKRs are tailored to each team member's career growth, interests, and well-being. They're not necessarily directly related to the team or larger organization goals.

Personal OKRs allow people to choose how to spend time outside their formal responsibilities. Examples include learning a new skill, studying for an exam, or improving public speaking. I've been in companies where even losing weight was accepted as an OKR—an employee was permitted to use paid company time to go out running around the office in the afternoons.

These efforts are certainly positive for the individual. Personal OKRs could help attract talent and improve engagement and retention. However, how they contribute to the organization's goals is sometimes debatable. It's up to you and the organization to decide if introducing personal OKRs is beneficial in your situation.

If business is thriving and plenty of resources are available, I would say it's worth trying them out. If you're in a start-up running against the clock to survive, clearly, it's not a good idea to let your engineers spend paid time learning a new language or exercising.

Avoid Using OKRs in Performance Evaluations

Using OKRs in performance evaluations can be problematic because they are designed to measure progress toward specific, often ambitious, collective goals, not necessarily individual contributions. OKRs are typically set for teams or organizations as a whole, with the intention of driving alignment and focus on initiatives. Engineers may feel under excessive pressure to meet these goals, even if external factors such as resource limitations or shifting priorities make those goals less achievable.

An engineer should not be negatively labeled for the team failing to meet OKRs. Performance evaluations should take into account factors beyond just goal completion, such as collaboration, problem-solving skills, innovation, and overall contribution. OKRs focus primarily on measurable outcomes, which don't fully capture these aspects of an engineer's work.

Another downside of tying OKRs to performance evaluations is that it may encourage individuals to set less ambitious goals or even game the system. If engineers are evaluated based on the number of OKRs achieved, they might reason, "Why not set the bar low?" For example, if the number of merged PRs is set as a team key result, engineers could be incentivized to fragment the code excessively and submit micro-PRs just to boost the count rather than focusing on delivering meaningful contributions.

Let your team come up with big, exciting goals without worrying about being punished for not reaching them later on.

Key Points

- Without clear goals, employees may lose motivation and struggle to understand how their work contributes to the broader vision.

- Objectives define the "what"—ambitious yet attainable goals that align with the organization's mission. Key results define the "how"—specific, measurable steps that track progress toward achieving the objective.

- Regularly review and document OKR progress through biweekly check-ins, one-on-ones, and transparent tools to maintain alignment and adaptability.

- Personal OKRs support team members' personal and professional development.

- OKRs should encourage ambition without fear of punishment for unmet goals; they are meant to drive focus, not measure individual performance.

CHAPTER 7

Deliver Impactful Projects

The ultimate goal of software development is to deliver value to the user. Achieving this requires collaboration among individuals from diverse disciplines, all brought together under the umbrella of a project. These disciplines range from product management and design to engineering, quality assurance, and support. Orchestrating this effort is the primary responsibility of project management.

Project management is a complex and demanding field, especially for large-scale initiatives. Project managers coordinate tasks, manage timelines, mitigate risks, update stakeholders, and keep the project on track and within budget.

However, project managers cannot do all these by themselves. They rely heavily on other leaders, including you, who represent the engineering team, to push the project forward and tackle the challenges that arise. Each discipline looks after its piece of the puzzle, ensuring the project is more than just a collection of tasks but a unified, cohesive solution.

As you surely know, a project generally has four major phases: planning, execution, delivery, and maintenance. In my experience, most problems start brewing in the planning phase, particularly when there is not enough of it. Here are some things I suggest you consider.

© Jonathan Sosa 2025
J. Sosa, *From Culture to Code*, Apress Pocket Guides,
https://doi.org/10.1007/979-8-8688-1428-0_7

Know What to Build

Typically, people involved have a rough idea of two things at the planning phase of a project: the product to build and the technology to use to build it. Perhaps, there is already a draft product specification, and the engineering team has decided on the programming language and framework to use or even a working prototype.

These two elements don't complete the picture. Before teams rush to break down the work into backlog tasks and start executing, two additional points need to be clarified for everyone: business motivation and constraints.

Business Motivation

What is the business intent behind this project? Is it to gain more customers, save costs, or improve the quality of an existing product? Understanding the exact motivation can help guide the right decisions throughout the process.

To make a vague concept like business motivation more tangible, start by defining clear success metrics. In simpler words, how will you know if the business motivation has been achieved? For example, if the motivation is to save costs, a success metric could be "20% less cloud infrastructure costs." You might have guessed by now, but this is the starting point of OKRs.

Without something concrete to aim for, it is impossible to know when a project is successful or even completed; teams lack a shared understanding of what they are working toward, leading to ambiguity, scope creep, and potentially endless iterations.

Constraints

How many people, time, and money are available to complete the project? Are there any regulations or compliance requirements you need to follow? Are there any technological limitations? What are the acceptance criteria?

In my experience, unforeseen constraints are the most common cause of delays because they tend to surface late in the project, sometimes even close to its delivery date. They might even force the team to return to the drawing board and scrap all the work done so far, demotivating everyone involved.

Assign Roles and Responsibilities

Clear project roles and responsibilities help the people involved move fast and reduce confusion about who's working on what, especially if you are part of a complex project with many decision-makers and subject matter experts.

A popular tool to identify and document the responsibilities within a project is the RACI chart, also known as the responsibility assignment matrix. Its name comes from the following four key roles:

- Responsible: The person doing the work. There should only be one Responsible role per task so you know who to go to with questions or updates.

- Accountable: The person ultimately delivering the work and responsible for signing off that it's done. In some situations, the same person could fill both the Responsible and Accountable roles.

- Consulted: People who are asked for their opinion. Multiple Consulted roles may exist for each task, project milestone, or deliverable.

- Informed: People who will be kept up to date on progress and completion of work.

Obviously, you don't need to list every task in the RACI chart. Instead, keep it high level by focusing on the project's major activities, phases, or deliverables. This approach simplifies the chart, making it easier to read and understand while effectively communicating team members' key responsibilities and roles. A simplified RACI chart is more flexible and easier to update as the project evolves.

The roles and responsibilities you assign to your engineers should align closely with the expectations outlined earlier in this book. While the engineer levels define high-level expectations, project responsibilities make these expectations tangible, specific, and actionable. Be deliberate in assigning work to your engineers, ensuring it supports their career growth. For instance, a senior engineer aspiring to reach the staff engineer level could benefit from taking on the role of technical lead for a large project. Challenging but achievable opportunities like this are what foster growth.

Define an Escalation Protocol

No project has ever gone according to its original plan. It is impossible to foresee everything that can go wrong, so expect the unexpected and be ready for it. Bad news must travel quickly and reach the right people.

An escalation protocol, simply put, is a predefined process that outlines how major obstacles and risks that cannot be resolved at the project team level are escalated to higher authorities. With this information, authorities can course-correct, add resources to the project, seek external help, or implement other measures to alleviate the situation.

When I joined Drivemode as VP of Engineering, a major project to build a software platform for electric motorbikes was entering its second year. I found mobility software development particularly challenging because it requires extensive coordination with hardware manufacturers. In our case, Honda designed and manufactured the bike's body, but other vendors were in charge of different components, such as the accelerometer and GPS unit.

As I familiarized myself with the project, I noticed the massive size of the development task backlog compared to the size of the engineering team. With the people we had, we could not complete the project by the given deadline. In the automotive industry, deadlines are a big deal; not meeting one means factories can't start manufacturing vehicles.

After many discussions, I had the project manager change the project's status to "In Risk of Delay" and promptly got to work. To address the issue, we brought in external contractors to help with development and negotiated to reduce the scope of the initial release.

Looking back, I wish I had a more accurate picture of the real project status when I joined. I would have acted sooner and saved precious time. Most people, myself included, don't like to deliver bad news. Nobody wants to ruin the party, but hiding from reality only makes things worse in the end.

You should promote a culture of welcoming bad news, where those who speak out and bring it to us are appreciated and even rewarded. The first step is to implement an escalation protocol: a document specifying who to notify, in a blameless way, when a major issue or risk is found.

Manage Complexity

Projects often fail due to inadequate requirements, ineffective planning, or poor management. However, when the failure is mainly technical, it is frequently because of excessive complexity. The software can become so intricate that no one fully understands its overall functionality. When a project reaches the point where no one foresees the impact of code changes in one area on other parts, progress comes to a standstill.

Computing legend Edsger Dijkstra pointed out in the early 1970s that no one's skull is big enough to contain a modern computer program. Therefore, software engineers shouldn't try to understand whole programs at once; instead, they should try to organize them so that they can safely focus on one part at a time.

At the software architecture level, a problem's complexity is managed by dividing the system into subsystems. The more independent the subsystems, the safer it is to focus on one aspect of complexity at a time. This independence minimizes the risk that changes in one subsystem will adversely affect others, leading to a more stable and reliable system overall. Make sure your team approaches development with this in mind.

This principle applies to all levels of software development and project management. Complex work should be broken down into smaller, digestible subtasks, making them easier to assign, track, and complete. This granular approach allows team members to make steady progress, provides a sense of accomplishment as each subtask is completed, and simplifies identifying issues early on.

I feel that the importance of breaking down complex tasks is often underestimated in some teams, even though it's a fundamental step in software development. The Agile framework suggests breaking down the work as a team during backlog refining (a.k.a. grooming) sessions. Still, in my opinion, having the whole team there is unnecessary and even wasteful. Most of the time, a product manager and tech lead is enough.

Similarly, project deliverables should be divided into shorter milestones. Establishing incremental goals helps maintain momentum and keeps the team focused on immediate objectives while progressing toward the larger vision. Shortened milestones enable frequent feedback cycles, allowing for adjustments based on stakeholder input or changing requirements.

I'm a big proponent of splitting projects into phases. The first phase is always the bare minimum scope that delivers value to the user as soon as possible. The second phase includes not only expanded functionality but also improvements based on user feedback from the first phase. The sooner you can put something in your user's hands, the better.

Help Manage the Backlog

Typically, the Product Owner is primarily responsible for managing the product backlog. The Product Owner acts as a bridge between customers and the development team, ensuring that the backlog accurately reflects the organization's priorities and objectives.

In smaller organizations, the CEO or President typically fulfills this role, while in larger companies, it is usually handled by the Head of Product or an equivalent position. Regardless of the official title, this role demands collaboration and close cooperation with engineering. It is crucial for you to thoroughly understand this role and be able to influence its decisions.

The Product Owner has two primary responsibilities at a high level: (1) decide what enters the backlog and its priority and (2) manage stakeholder expectations—both are collaborative efforts where you need to be deeply engaged.

Simply put, the Product Owner decides what enters the backlog based on the organization's objectives. The process begins by gathering and prioritizing input from stakeholders, including customers and internal leaders, including you, to ensure that the most impactful and achievable items are addressed first.

Evaluate each potential backlog entry, taking into account technical considerations such as complexity, dependencies, risks, resource availability, and team skillset. Can the team implement this? Is it technically feasible? How much time would we need? Items not meeting these criteria can be deferred or removed from the backlog.

Always remain vigilant—letting an item into the backlog is a form of commitment. Requests come from all directions, and there is always more than the team can handle. Sometimes, the Product Owner will need your help managing stakeholder expectations and justifying declining requests.

When called upon to give your technical opinion about what makes it to the backlog and what doesn't, keep the following in mind:

- Remain honest about what is possible and maintain an open dialogue.

- Understand your team's capabilities and development velocity.

- Document your team's estimations and justify them with data.

- Assess and communicate technical risks in backlog candidates.

- It is perfectly acceptable to take time to gather information and form an opinion.

In the past, my eagerness to make a meaningful impact and be a good team player pushed me to say yes to opportunities and overcommit. While well-intentioned, taking more than my team and I could take often stretched our capacity and lowered our focus on the things that mattered the most.

Key Points

- Define success metrics to create a shared understanding of what constitutes project completion and success.

- Assign responsibilities to team members in ways that align with their career growth and support team development.

- Create a culture that welcomes reporting of bad news promptly and blamelessly to address risks early.

- Break down complex tasks into smaller, manageable subtasks to simplify tracking and execution.

- Advocate for focus and avoid overcommitment by prioritizing items that align with team capabilities and organizational goals.

CHAPTER 8

Adopt Best Practices

Best practices are essentially the gold standards within a particular field, established through experience, research, and consistent outcomes. They contain the collective wisdom and lessons learned from past efforts. You can bypass the trial-and-error phase and instead efficiently implement frameworks, methodologies, and processes that have already been validated for success. In simpler words, stand on the shoulders of giants.

Best practices also make it easier to scale: New engineers can study and internalize them to rapidly ramp up and start contributing. It helps new hires integrate seamlessly with the existing team, adhering to established workflows, coding standards, and development methodologies from day one.

Some methodologies tend to rise and fall in popularity as industry trends evolve, which is why I hesitate to label them as best practices. Their fleeting nature suggests they are more about responding to the current zeitgeist than providing universally applicable solutions. Take your time to assess them and avoid wasting resources chasing the latest industry fad.

Decide How "Agile" You Want to Be

I intentionally place "Agile" in quotation marks because this methodology is often subject to various interpretations and implementations. Since its inception in 2001, Agile has evolved and been adapted in numerous ways. Despite its long history, it is often misunderstood as a one-size-fits-all solution.

© Jonathan Sosa 2025
J. Sosa, *From Culture to Code*, Apress Pocket Guides,
https://doi.org/10.1007/979-8-8688-1428-0_8

As a certified Agile Scrum Master and Product Owner, I generally advocate for the Agile methodology with some reservations. My support is rooted in the belief that it can significantly enhance an organization's effectiveness when properly implemented. However, the actual value of Agile is realized only when it is tailored to fit each organization's unique needs.

In a nutshell, the Agile Manifesto emphasizes a flexible and collaborative approach to software development by prioritizing individuals over processes and tools, delivering working software over comprehensive documentation, fostering customer collaboration over strict contract negotiation, and embracing change rather than rigidly adhering to a plan. I recommend you look at the Agile principles at https://agilemanifesto. org/principles.html for a more in-depth explanation.

Notice how this summary conveys a sense of "move fast; we'll figure things out as we go." It emphasizes prioritizing rapid progress and iterative development over exhaustive upfront planning. You should first consider how well the Agile methodology suits your organization by looking at factors like the nature and complexity of your project, the level of uncertainty in your environment, and the industry's particularities. And by "you," I mean not only the engineering team but also other departments involved in software development, such as product management and design.

For instance, in fast-paced industries like technology startups, following Agile to the letter can be highly effective in capitalizing on emerging opportunities and staying ahead of competitors. Conversely, in sectors that require strict compliance, extensive documentation, or high precision—such as healthcare, automotive, or aerospace—a more structured approach, like Waterfall, might be better to enforce safety, accuracy, and regulatory adherence.

While this might be controversial, I view Agile as a flexible framework rather than a strict mandate. You don't need to adhere 100% to it. Instead, you can adopt a hybrid approach by incorporating only the best elements in your situation.

When I was working on navigation software for electric vehicles, we had to adapt our development schedule to align our deliverables with the vehicle's quality control and manufacturing milestones. Missing a critical deadline or delivering software with a serious bug could cause factories to halt their production lines, resulting in costly delays.

Furthermore, transportation laws mandate the inclusion of specific safety features and strict performance requirements. For example, the speedometer must be shown to the user within a few seconds after turning the vehicle on. These are essential components of the project scope; without them, the vehicle cannot be sold. As you can imagine, we couldn't adopt Agile as is: we needed more structure, documentation, and thoughtful planning than what the Agile methodology suggests.

Common Agile Pitfalls

If you decide to adopt the Agile methodology partially or entirely, you should be aware of the following common pitfalls:

- Insufficient training and lack of guidance. Without a knowledgeable guide, teams may struggle to understand and implement Agile principles correctly.

- Using Agile as an excuse for poor planning and ever-changing requirements. Effective planning requires foresight, goals, and milestones regardless of the methodology.

- Excessive meetings—such as daily stand-ups, weekly sprint planning sessions, retrospectives, and backlog refinement meetings—can cause meeting fatigue.

- Using story points based on complexity while expecting estimations based on time. Ultimately, the business needs to understand the expected delivery date, so complexity is not a useful estimation method, in my view.

- Failing to incorporate feedback from team members about how things are working under Agile.

Use a Task Management Tool

Task management tools are a central hub for organizing and prioritizing work. They allow engineers to list all their responsibilities and arrange them in logical order while considering dependencies. Project managers can use them to identify bottlenecks and adjust priorities as needed. Engineering managers can rely on them to balance their engineers' workload and measure overall progress.

There are many good alternatives out there. I encourage you to compare them and pick the one that works best for you, but remember, these tools are helpful only if everyone puts the time and effort into them. They must be configured to reflect the team's workflow, tickets prioritized and well-written, and their status updated daily. I strongly believe it is worth the effort.

When I joined Mercari back in early 2019, they weren't using anything to manage the development work. Product managers would sit with designers and engineers and tell them more or less what to implement. The engineers would implement it and return to show how it was going. This approach was fine for simple cosmetic changes but chaos for more complex features requiring involvement from multiple people. There was no coordination or visibility into who was doing what, and delivery timelines were missed.

When I started promoting task management tools, I encountered resistance. Some people considered it an unnecessary overhead: "Why spend time writing tickets when we could be writing code?" So, it took me a while to collect evidence of its usefulness, socialize it, and convince the rest of the engineering and product teams to use it. We conducted a month-long pilot limited to one project to see how it worked for us. The benefits were evident not only to management but also to individual contributors.

After the pilot, we hired a Technical Program Manager who not only had mastery of management tools but also knew how to configure and adapt them to our ways of work. Specifically:

- Types of tasks: Epic, Story, Task, Subtask, and Spike

- Task statuses: Discarded, Ready for Development, In Development, In Code Review, In QA, QA Feedback Given, Ready for Release, and Done

- Restrictions on what status could come after another based on the team's workflow

- Automation that changes a task's status based on an external event, like a PR merge

- Automated reports for management to visualize project progress, workloads, and where the resources were being invested

Fortunately, after a few months, everyone was onboard and never looked back.

Define Code Review Guidelines

Pull request (PR) review is one of the fundamental processes of software engineering. It supports the writing of high-quality, future-proof, and maintainable code. You must ensure team guidelines are in place for effective code reviews.

Even the most experienced software engineers can make poor choices, and code review is an opportunity to get feedback from others with fresh eyes. Reviewers may also need more context and make incorrect assumptions. Both of these are normal and should not negatively reflect on the individuals.

Promoting quick code reviews is important for unblocking other team members. A review may take multiple iterations, making this even more important. Most PRs should be reviewed within a few hours—authors should remind reviewers if their PRs go unnoticed for more than 24 hours.

Reviews aim to provide constructive, actionable feedback to improve the quality of the code. There is never any reason for a comment to be harsh. Personal attacks must not be tolerated.

Here are some pointers to look out for when reviewing a PR:

- Does the PR address one single feature or issue?

- Is the code easy to understand? Is it evident what it does?

- If technical debt is introduced, does it have a TODO explaining its reason?

- Does the code follow established architecture and style standards?

- Is the code efficient? Is there any duplicated logic?

The most common issue I encounter when operationalizing review guidelines is that PRs take too long to review. In most cases, this arises simply because the assigned reviewer doesn't have notifications enabled. The solution is straightforward: you can configure review request notifications to be sent via text message.

If notifications are received but ignored, it could indicate a problem with your engineering culture. Reinforce with your team that reviewing PRs is a high-priority task—potentially more important than whatever the reviewer was working on when the request came through. Stale PRs not only block progress but are also prone to merge conflicts, which causes more work for the author later on.

If your team takes too long to review PRs, you can set an OKR to track and shorten the average time it takes for a PR to be merged. It's a concrete goal and easily measured. I recommend aiming for a 30~40 hour range. There are plenty of tools that can automatically retrieve this data from code repository systems.

Define Communication Guidelines

Meetings

Unnecessary meetings are a common source of frustration in the workplace, particularly among engineers who need uninterrupted time to focus on complex tasks. You are responsible for protecting your team from the productivity drain caused by such meetings.

Jason Fried and David Heinemeier Hansson go as far as saying that unnecessary meetings are toxic in their book *Rework*: "When you think about it, the true cost of meetings is staggering. Let's say you're going to schedule a meeting that lasts one hour, and you invite ten people to attend. That's actually a ten-hour meeting, not a one-hour meeting. You're trading ten hours of productivity for one hour of meeting time."

Based on my experience, I feel most meetings can be avoided by enhancing documentation practices and promoting asynchronous communication. Still, when they are unavoidable, it is crucial to get the most out of them. Here are some strategies:

- Meetings have a designated facilitator responsible for moving the conversation forward and ensuring the attendees stay on topic. By default, the meeting organizer is the facilitator.

- Meetings have a designated notetaker who documents the critical discussion points, decisions, and next steps. Ideally, this should be someone other than the facilitator.

- The facilitator shares information about the meeting beforehand so the attendees can review it and come ready with questions.

- Meetings have a description, including their context and goals.

- Meeting invites, particularly for recurring meetings, have a link to the meeting log document on the calendar invite. Meeting minutes are important for visibility to outside attendees.

- Meeting attendees are kept to a minimum. The more people who join, the more likely the meeting will fail to achieve its goal.

- If the goal of a meeting is to reach a decision, the person(s) with decision-making power are present.

That said, meetings can have a positive impact on interpersonal relationships regardless of their objective. Regardless of the meeting's primary objective, the mere act of coming together fosters a sense of connection among team members. These interactions create opportunities for colleagues to share perspectives, understand each other's working styles, and build trust over time. If you work in a remote team, perhaps promoting more meetings is the way to go.

Online Messaging

Most communication nowadays happens online in messaging applications. This medium has nuances and challenges, such as the potential for miscommunication due to the absence of nonverbal cues, information overload from constant notifications, and the blurring of boundaries between work and personal life.

Managing these challenges requires documenting and promoting clear guidelines. Here are my suggestions:

- Create and use appropriate channels: Create suitable channels to keep conversations organized and ensure the right audience sees them.

- Be clear and concise: Use clear, straightforward language and get to the point quickly. Utilize bullet points or numbered lists for better readability.

- Respect availability: Be aware of team members' time zones and working hours. Avoid sending nonurgent messages late at night or during weekends. Understand that excessive notifications can disrupt others' workflows.

- Use threads: Reply in threads to maintain context and reduce clutter.

- Be responsive: A quick reaction shows engagement even if you need more time to respond.

- Provide context: Include links, screenshots, and other necessary details in your messages to facilitate understanding.

- Promote equal participation: Include all team members in conversations and avoid inside jokes or references that may exclude others.

Additionally, you should be mindful that emotionally charged online messages can quickly escalate into arguments. This happens for two reasons: (1) Some people are friendly and respectful in person but sometimes harsh online. (2) Text is easily misinterpreted as it lacks nonverbal communication components, like tone of voice and body language.

Text is an inherently impersonal medium, often lacking the nuance and emotional context conveyed through tone of voice or body language. As a result, even something as seemingly harmless as a smiley emoji can be misinterpreted as sarcasm—especially when negative emotions or tensions are involved. If you see this happening, quickly transition the discussion to a video call or in-person meeting. These formats provide opportunities for more precise communication, allowing participants to express themselves fully and resolve misunderstandings.

It's also important to keep an eye on emojis, especially in multicultural environments where their interpretations can vary. Certain symbols or gestures represented by emojis may carry different meanings, potentially resulting in misunderstandings or unintentional offense.

Once, one of my engineers complained about a colleague reacting to one of their messages with an emoji of Pepe the Frog. Pepe the Frog was originally an inoffensive comic character created by cartoonist Matt Furie, but later, in 2015, it was appropriated as a symbol of the alt-right movement and further associated with hate speech. The person using this emoji wasn't aware of all this—they just saw a funny little frog face. Ultimately, we decided to remove Pepe, and since then, a compliance team has reviewed the emoji catalog quarterly.

Communication in Multicultural Environments

I've been fortunate to work in some of Tokyo's most culturally diverse companies throughout my career. I've noticed that most people from all over the world who come to live in Japan tend to prefer multicultural workplaces. I suspect this is because it is difficult to master the Japanese language and the communication style.

Putting language aside, the difference in communication styles between cultures lies in how much they rely on context—high-context versus low-context. No culture is completely high-context or low-context; rather, it sits on a gradient.

In cultures with low-context communication styles, like the United States, people assume little implicit knowledge linking the speaker and the listener. In low-context countries, effective communication must be simple, clear, and explicit to pass the message. They are typically task-based and not afraid of being direct.

In contrast, in high-context countries like Japan, people tend to communicate implicitly and rely heavily on shared context. They rely on relationships and avoid confrontation as much as possible. The speaker often expects the listener to understand what is being said with few words.

Someone from a high-context culture might accuse a low-context speaker of being too direct, whereas a low-context listener might often wonder if the high-context speaker will ever get the point across. Needless to say, this difference in style breeds misunderstandings.

For example, I've observed that silence often becomes a point of misunderstanding in meetings between Japanese and American counterparts. For the Japanese, silence is a tool for reflection and a way to create space for others to contribute. However, Americans may interpret silence as a lack of engagement or disinterest. For Americans, silence is uncomfortable; for Japanese, it's not.

In her book *The Culture Map: Breaking Through the Invisible Boundaries of Global Business*, Erin Meyer suggests listening actively to what is meant instead of what is being said when working with people from high-context cultures. She advises putting in the effort to "read the room" by observing nonverbal cues and emotional states, which can provide valuable additional context to the conversation.

Conversely, if you find yourself working with individuals from lower-context cultures, Meyer recommends being as transparent, clear, and specific as possible. It's perfectly acceptable to be verbose and take the time to articulate details thoroughly. Don't assume the receiver of the communication knows what you know.

Key Points

- Avoid blindly following industry fads; assess their relevance and fit for your organization before implementation.

- Agile can be powerful but isn't one-size-fits-all; adapt it to your project's complexity, industry requirements, and organizational culture.

- Project management tools centralize task organization, prioritize work, and improve visibility for all stakeholders.

- Limit unnecessary meetings, provide clear agendas, and use meeting logs to maximize productivity.

- Be mindful of cultural communication differences, balancing explicit clarity for low-context cultures and nuanced understanding for high-context ones.

CHAPTER 9

Build Software Right

In construction, establishing a solid foundation is essential to secure the structural integrity of the entire building. Without it, the walls would sink and crumble under the ceiling's weight. Similarly, in software development, it's important to invest in a strong foundation before developing the required functionality. How good your foundation is influences both software quality and delivery speed.

In my experience, jumping straight into building features without a proper foundation often gives a false sense of progress. When stakeholders see a partially functional version of the software, it can create the illusion that things are moving forward quickly and work is getting done. However, this apparent immediate progress can be misleading. Without taking the time to properly architect and build the basics, there's a likelihood of ending with inconsistent and poorly structured code, duplicated efforts, difficult bugs, and performance issues that only become apparent later in the development cycle. Essentially, while it might seem like you're advancing, rushing into feature development often results in more work down the road.

I urge you to avoid taking such shortcuts. They will inevitably slow your team down as they become bogged down with fixing bugs and refactoring low-quality code. So, in reality, you're just borrowing from the future. Stakeholders usually realize they are in this bad situation too late when it's more expensive to correct.

© Jonathan Sosa 2025
J. Sosa, *From Culture to Code*, Apress Pocket Guides,
https://doi.org/10.1007/979-8-8688-1428-0_9

I've had bad experiences joining projects in their last phases and been unpleasantly surprised. On the surface, the product appeared to be "almost done," but after digging in, I noticed it didn't support edge cases, had hard-coded data, wasn't performant enough, and was bug-ridden. It had a lot of hidden work left to do.

Following, you'll find what I recommend doing at the beginning of new development projects, particularly those of significant size.

Choose the Tech Stack

The tech stack you choose will significantly shape your organization's future, serving as the foundation for all your software development efforts. It will influence hiring decisions, as certain technologies require specialized skills, affecting the pool of candidates you can attract and retain. A modern and widely used tech stack can make your organization more appealing to top talent, while a niche or outdated stack might limit your ability to find the right engineers.

Additionally, the chosen stack directly impacts development speed; efficient tools and frameworks can accelerate development, enabling your team to iterate quickly and bring products to market faster. This agility is crucial in a landscape where time-to-market determines your organization's success.

The first thing to choose is the programming language. Engineers are more productive using a familiar language than an unfamiliar one, and some languages are better at certain applications than others. For example, Python has become popular in data science and machine learning due to its simplicity and readability, allowing data scientists and researchers to focus on the problem instead of syntax. Golang, designed by Google, is a great choice for large-scale back-end applications thanks to its optimized machine code compilation and built-in concurrency capabilities.

You should avoid picking based on an engineer's personal preference or what's trendy. Selecting technologies solely because certain team members favor them or are currently popular can result in significant challenges down the road, like an underperforming product or an inability to hire engineers.

I've observed situations where code bases become tangled messes due to the introduction of multiple redundant frameworks that perform similar functions. Situations like these happen when each new engineer brings in their preferred tech without considering the existing architecture or the overall implications for the team. Remain vigilant and make it clear to your team that new tech needs to be assessed and vouched for.

You and your team must thoroughly assess new technology before committing to it. The elements I typically look for are the following:

- Product fit: Is the technology compatible with the product you will build? Is it performant enough to serve the expected number of users?

- Maturity: Is the technology proven and well-established? Are there successful products built with it?

- Knowledge base: Is there enough technical documentation available? Are there code examples, books, articles, and tutorials on the technology?

- Support: Is there an organization or large community behind the technology? Can you get help with technical issues, either free or paid?

- Talent availability: Is your team experienced in the technology? If not, is there enough talent available in the job market?

Regardless of how trendy or attractive a technology might appear, without proper assessment, you risk wasting your team's time on development that may ultimately be ineffective and require significant reworking. New technologies often promise enhanced performance, increased efficiency, or innovative features, making them appealing on the surface. However, their adoption can provoke unforeseen challenges without carefully evaluating how well they align with your situation.

I prefer to avoid new, unfamiliar technologies unless there is a strong reason. Their lack of support and proven track record can result in prolonged problems and increased maintenance efforts, stealing resources from delivering features. On top, the team will likely need weeks, perhaps months, to get familiarized with them.

Multiplatform Frameworks

Java's slogan from the 1990s, "Write Once, Run Anywhere," famously morphed into the joke "Write Once, Debug Everywhere," highlighting the often unfulfilled promises of multiplatform frameworks. It encapsulated developers' frustration when code that worked on one platform behaved unpredictably on another, requiring extensive debugging.

Technology has come a long way since then, with significant advancements in both hardware and software. However, we still encounter challenges related to performance optimization, platform-specific features, and user experience. Cross-platform tools often involve trade-offs, such as larger application sizes or reduced performance compared to native applications. In addition, keeping up with the rapid evolution of platforms can introduce serious compatibility issues.

If you're considering using a multiplatform framework for your application, keep your expectations in check. At a high level, a project's total cost can be divided into the upfront and maintenance phases. The upfront phase is the development of the first version of the software, while the maintenance phase lasts the whole software life cycle. In my experience, multiplatform frameworks significantly reduce the upfront cost but add to the maintenance cost due to the extra complexities. Notably:

- Continuous integration pipelines are more complicated and break more often.

- There is less technical documentation and support available than native platforms.

- Debugging is more difficult due to the inscrutable code generated by the framework.

- The additional layer often introduces issues that are hard to resolve on some platforms.

I believe consistency is the most significant advantage of a multiplatform approach, not cost savings. Sharing a single code base keeps feature parity and almost uniform behavior across them. Additionally, a unified code base allows the team to share expertise more effectively. This shared knowledge base leads to more efficient development processes and a more cohesive team dynamic.

When deciding if multiplatform is right for you, ask yourself these questions:

- What to optimize for? Save time and money, reduce risk, or have a consistent product?

- Is someone in your team an expert in the multiplatform framework? If not, is someone ready to become one?

- Are the native engineers already in your team open to retooling their skill sets?

- Is the multiplatform framework adequate for my performance and security requirements?

Don't Use Prototypes As a Starting Point

Prototypes are developed primarily to validate a concept, assess feasibility, or demonstrate functionality to stakeholders. Building them is fun because they typically do not have restrictions or limitations, allowing for creative freedom and experimentation.

However, a common mistake I've seen is attempting to evolve a prototype into a market-ready product. Prototypes are inherently designed to be temporary solutions. Once they have fulfilled their role, prototypes are meant to be discarded. They are not built with the intention of meeting the demands of a production environment, such as scalability, performance, extensibility, and sustainability.

During the prototyping phase, decision-making is often concentrated in the hands of one or two engineers who drive the development process. This centralized decision-making can lead to a lack of broader team input, as other team members don't have the opportunity to offer their perspectives or expertise. As a result, the decisions might not entirely reflect the collective insights or address the diverse needs of the entire team. This scenario can create friction and disagreement among team members who feel excluded from decision-making.

I recommend initiating a new repository once a prototype has fulfilled its purpose and you are ready to move into the product development phase. While you can reference the code from the prototype, avoid copying it into the product code base as is.

Set Coding Standards

Coding standards dictate how code should be written, formatted, and organized within a code base. These standards encompass various aspects of coding, including syntax, naming conventions, file organization, commenting practices, and architectural patterns.

By establishing and adhering to coding standards from the beginning of the project, your team can ensure that the code base remains consistent, readable, and maintainable, regardless of the number of contributors or code base size. A code base with standards makes it easier for engineers to navigate the code and contribute to different areas consistently. It also helps new engineers onboard quickly.

I recommend that engineers with seniority lead the formulation of the coding standards while ensuring that the entire team has the opportunity to provide feedback and refine them. This inclusive approach not only leverages the diverse perspectives and experiences within the team but also fosters a sense of ownership. Engineers tend to respect the standards they helped create more than the ones someone else decided and imposed on them.

Static code analysis tools like linters, style checkers, and complexity analyzers can help you enforce the standards automatically. Use them as your code base gatekeepers by running them on all new code before it gets merged into the main branch.

Another notable advantage of well-defined code standards is the reduction in cognitive load for your engineers, as they remove much of the uncertainty that might otherwise arise when deciding on naming conventions, architectural patterns, or formatting details. Instead of expending mental energy on these routine decisions, your people can rely on the standards as a guiding framework.

Coding standards are intended to evolve as development progresses. Inevitably, discoveries and new insights will render some initial decisions inappropriate or outdated. You might also encounter new issues that can be prevented with additional rules. Have your team regularly revisit them to incorporate new technologies, methodologies, and lessons learned from ongoing projects.

Configure Continuous Integration, Continuous Delivery (CI/CD)

A CI/CD pipeline automates delivering code from an engineer's computer to a usable software package. This includes a code review process, static and security checks, compilation, test automation, integration, and deployment to test and production environments.

Implementing a CI/CD pipeline from the beginning of the project helps enforce coding standards and guarantees a baseline level of quality across the code base. Engineers can maintain consistency and reduce the likelihood of introducing bugs.

Moreover, a well-established pipeline facilitates rapid iteration by continuously delivering software to stakeholders as it is being developed. New code automatically gets built and delivered to the engineering team, QA, and other interested parties. This allows everyone to understand the actual progress of development and share feedback. As a result, development cycles become more efficient, and the team can respond promptly to changing requirements or issues.

CI/CD pipelines are considered part of the infrastructure and should be managed following Infrastructure as Code (IaC) practices. IaC allows you to define the desired state of your infrastructure in a declarative or imperative format using configuration files, which can be stored in version control systems like Git. This enables versioning, collaboration, and rollback capabilities.

Keep in mind that maintaining a CI/CD pipeline requires consistent effort and attention. Updates to its dependencies or changes to your code base can potentially break the pipeline, disrupting your workflow. To mitigate these risks, I suggest that all engineers on the team become familiar with it and acquire the expertise necessary to troubleshoot and fix issues. Even if you have a dedicated DevOps team, you should avoid situations where only a few engineers are in charge of them.

Pipelines for mobile applications are typically more fragile because they deliver packages to Apple's App Store and Google Play Store for distribution. The app stores frequently update their requirements and guidelines, which can change unexpectedly and break the pipeline.

Additionally, I suggest you set up monitoring on all your pipelines to notify the team when something fails. I've experienced situations where people don't notice they are using an old software version because it silently failed to build the latest source code.

Start with the Building Blocks

In all software projects, there are common components are used across the code base. Think of them as Lego pieces to be assembled into functional artifacts. The quality of these pieces and how well they fit together can significantly affect the development speed and overall software quality.

When starting a new project, I suggest focusing on defining and building these foundational components first. Investing time upfront to design and implement high-quality common components pays dividends in the long run. It reduces duplication of effort, minimizes bugs, enforces consistency, and simplifies testing and debugging processes. As the application grows and requirements change, well-defined building blocks make it easier to modify existing features, add new functionality, or refactor parts of the code base.

Moreover, having robust building blocks in place enables different team members to work in parallel with a shared understanding of the code foundation. New hires can ramp up quicker, too, by studying the well-structured pieces and their accompanying documentation rather than navigating ad hoc code.

UI Components

If your software includes a user interface, build a catalog of UI components your team can use repeatedly across the application. This catalog should contain common elements like color palettes, buttons, menus, input fields, and typography.

Creating these components in a centralized repository allows your team to accelerate the development process and maintain uniformity and consistency across all screens in your application. It also promotes collaboration between designers and engineers, as everyone has access to the same set of standardized components, fostering a cohesive design language.

When design standards evolve, changes can be made in one place and propagated automatically across the entire application, ensuring consistency. Designers can propose improvements without worrying too much about the engineering cost. This approach also enhances scalability, allowing your application to grow seamlessly as new features are added.

API Clients

If your application likely consumes APIs to retrieve and modify data from the server, I suggest you build a centralized catalog of API clients at the very beginning of the project to simplify maintenance and scalability as your application grows. When the API specifications change, having a single client means you only need to update the client in one location, reducing the effort required to keep up with new versions.

Moreover, consider implementing an abstraction layer between your API clients and the application logic. This abstraction layer can decouple your application's core logic from the underlying API implementation, making your code base more flexible and future-proof. For example, you can have an abstract client for user authentication that utilizes Google's Firebase API client and later replace it with another authentication provider with minimal changes to your application logic.

State Management

Implement a standard way to retrieve and save application state data. Depending on its purpose, the data can be categorized as global, such as authenticated user information accessible throughout the entire application, or local, such as a list of products displayed on a catalog page.

This standardization not only simplifies development and debugging but also enhances the overall reliability and user experience by ensuring that state data is accurately and consistently managed throughout the application.

Error Handling

Errors should be presented to users consistently, taking into account their severity and the actions required to address them. Whether you use toasts, pop-ups, or inline messages, having a dedicated error mechanism readily available eliminates guesswork and enforces uniform error handling across your application. Additionally, this consistency enhances the user experience by providing clear and predictable feedback.

If the software you're building has a UI, you'll need to work with designers to determine how to show errors based on their severity and cause, among other factors. For example, perhaps you want to show an error caused by invalid user input differently than an internal system error—the former is actionable, but the latter isn't.

Observability

Observability refers to the ability to measure a system's internal states based on its external outputs. It is typically defined by three main pillars: logs, metrics, and traces. Information collected by these subsystems is critical to detect and diagnose performance bottlenecks, bugs, security vulnerabilities, and other potential issues.

I consider observability a fundamental building block because it helps unearth issues early on that might otherwise go undetected. For instance, a complex database query might perform well in the development environment but significantly degrade system performance once the software is subjected to real-world user traffic.

Observability also includes business metrics: monthly active users, click rates, etc., but those can be introduced at a later stage of the project.

Manage Technical Debt

Technical debt is akin to taking out a loan to accelerate a purchase. Imagine you urgently need a car and decide to buy a less expensive model with a high-interest loan instead of saving for a higher-quality vehicle. You get the car immediately, fulfilling your immediate need, but over time, the high-interest payments accumulate, making the total cost much higher than if paid without a loan.

Excessive technical debt makes your code bases riskier and more expensive to maintain, slowing down your team and resulting in lower quality and longer time to market. However, technical debt is the price of doing business—it is inevitable and expected. Your job is to manage and keep it under control, not try to avoid it altogether. You must be able to seize opportunities and deliver business value even if it temporarily negatively affects the quality of your code base.

Sometimes, what appears to be technical debt is the result of external constraints, such as government regulations. For example, the General Data Protection Regulation in the EU requires strict data segregation, prohibiting the storage of multiple types of personally identifying data in the same database table. From a software design perspective, this is inefficient, and someone without the context would immediately point it out.

Beware of engineers who confuse technical debt with code that doesn't match their personal preferences. I've seen instances where, after a big refactor, the code is no more efficient or easier to work with than it was before. It's just different, and even worse, no one besides the refactorer knows it as well anymore.

You'll likely encounter some engineers who strongly oppose introducing additional technical debt. Throughout my career, I have been involved in heated debates between those who fiercely try to preserve the quality of the code base at all costs and those who prioritize making a business impact. Unfortunately, there is no straightforward way to decide which side to take. Evaluate each situation on a case-by-case basis, ultimately coming down to one question: Is the short-term benefit worth the long-term cost of repaying the technical debt with interest?

When you find yourself in a similar situation and decide to incur technical debt, it's important to address the engineers' concerns and explain to them the reasoning behind the decision. Pull requests with technical debt should be documented accordingly so the reviewers can understand the context and let the new, nonideal code enter the code base.

Pay Off Technical Debt

Paying off technical debt is a continuous team effort—it should not be the responsibility of one or two engineers. You should be ready to reserve a percentage of your team's capacity to address it.

The Scandinavian study *Software Developer Productivity Loss Due to Technical Debt* revealed that developers, on average, waste 23% of their time due to technical debt. To put it in perspective, this is more than one day per week.

In a more extreme case, in 2018, Stripe published data showing that engineers spend 42% of their time dealing with technical debt and bad code, almost half of their work capacity.

I can't give you a precise formula for calculating technical debt, but these are some signs that you might have too much of it:

- New features take too long to deliver.

- Estimates are often missed.

- A significant amount of unplanned work and surprises.

- Recurring bugs that are very difficult to fix.

- Low engineer morale.

It is your responsibility to convey the importance of these efforts to the organization and secure time to address them. A good approach is estimating the Return on Investment (ROI) based on three elements:

- Time to market: How much faster can you accelerate delivery with less technical debt?

- Quality impact: How few bugs will you have, and how much will that impact customer satisfaction?

- Motivational boost: How much would developer productivity increase through the motivational boost of no longer having to deal with so much technical debt?

Depending on your seniority, you might have to convince your superiors. If this is the case, like any other proposal, prepare the materials to back up your claims. In general, people like to see concrete numbers rather than hearing anecdotes. For example, instead of saying, "Tech debt is slowing development down," you could share more specifics like "We have 10% duplicated code" or "CI/CD build time is above 1 hour."

Once you get the green light, it's time to execute. The best times to focus for long periods on paying back technical debt are right after a big release and before the holidays. This is when business activity typically slows down, and the engineers can focus on refactoring and addressing issues.

I like using these opportunities to organize dedicated refactoring and bug-fixing marathons for my team. I turn them into events, announcing them to the organization to build anticipation and support. During these marathons, the engineers focus exclusively on improving the code bases—eliminating technical debt, optimizing performance, and addressing long-standing bugs. The duration typically spans one to two weeks, depending on the time available. I often incorporate incentives such as prizes or recognition for outstanding contributions to make it more engaging.

Rewriting from Scratch

All code is temporary. Some code bases are too outdated and ridden with technical debt, so the best course of action might be to rewrite them from scratch.

Starting from zero is always fun for engineers. They get to pick the tech stack, architecture, and code practices. They get a chance to *do it right* this time, for sure. They aren't like the dumb engineers who made the old code base, right?

The truth is, they'll make their own mistakes in the new code base. Rewriting from scratch doesn't guarantee the new code will be much better. Keep your expectations in check and look deeply into what the engineers tell you. Take the time to understand the true benefits to the business.

In my career, I've led the rewrite of three significant code bases, each with millions of users. Two of them were websites, and one was a mobile app.

Websites can be rewritten and released in phases, allowing you to redirect pages to the new code base as progress is made. This phased approach is both a blessing and a potential curse. A gradual migration often carries less urgency since the site remains functional even if work pauses midway. This may result in the rewrite project being deprioritized or even canceled to give space for other initiatives, leaving you stuck with two code bases, which is much worse.

On the other hand, mobile apps need to be compiled and delivered as one package, so the phased approach typically doesn't work. Unless the rewrite is complete, you have nothing to show for it. You need to go all the way. This requires upfront resource commitment and thoughtful planning.

I don't have extensive experience rewriting back-end services myself, but from what I've observed and learned, these projects can be more complex than rewriting websites or mobile applications. While it's true that you can often replace service endpoints incrementally without affecting the user experience, the real challenge lies in migrating data safely.

Data migration introduces several layers of complexity. It requires ensuring data integrity and maintaining compatibility between the old and new systems. Furthermore, migrating data in a live system increases the risk of downtime or performance degradation, as ongoing operations must be balanced with the migration process.

Even if you and your team are convinced to do a rewrite, you need to secure buy-in from the broader organization. Most rewrites require significant resources, which can impact other initiatives. Additionally, you may need to freeze the current code base, temporarily pausing new feature development, which could negatively affect business objectives.

The technical benefits alone aren't enough to secure organizational buy-in for a rewrite. To justify the effort, you must demonstrate the business impact by presenting projected metrics, such as increased user satisfaction and development velocity. Of course, these are only estimates; the real impact can only be seen when the rewrite is complete.

Key Points

- Avoid rushing into feature development. A robust foundation ensures better software quality, maintainability, and efficient delivery in the long run.

- Select a tech stack based on its fit for the product, maturity, support, and talent availability rather than personal preferences or trends.

- Establish coding standards for consistency and maintainability, involving the team to ensure buy-in and adaptability.

- Create reusable components, such as UI libraries, API clients, and state management patterns, to streamline development and maintain consistency.

- Technical debt is inevitable and sometimes necessary to meet business needs. It is important to schedule a time to address it.

CHAPTER 10

Choose Quality

Today, it's easy to become overwhelmed by a never-ending list of things to do. Constantly appearing busy has become a badge of honor in the hustle culture. However, high-quality, impactful work rarely stems from sheer busyness with many tasks. Instead, it results from deep, focused attention on a few priorities.

The term productivity is often mistakenly associated with the quantity of output one can produce. I believe this perspective comes from the Industrial Revolution, a time when productivity was measured primarily by the number of widgets manufactured. Perhaps its roots go even deeper, tracing back to agriculture, where productivity was gauged by how much food a farmer could yield from their land. This method of measuring productivity has a human cost. Pushing workers to optimize and try to perform every movement with maximum speed creates stress and exhaustion.

Software engineering is evidently very different from agriculture and manufacturing. Engineers are knowledge workers. Their mission is to transform knowledge into software with market value. As you know, the market value does not correlate with the size of the software program. Similarly, the value of your work is not dependent on quantity but rather on the quality of its outcome.

One of my favorite books, *Slow Productivity: The Lost Art of Accomplishment Without Burnout,* by Cal Newport, advocates for a more deliberate and sustainable approach to work. It challenges the modern

J. Sosa, *From Culture to Code*, Apress Pocket Guides,
https://doi.org/10.1007/979-8-8688-1428-0_10

emphasis on constant busyness and rapid output. It introduces the concept of "slow productivity," which promotes meaningful contributions at a sustainable pace, aiming to reduce burnout and enhance the quality of work.

Newport critiques the prevailing productivity culture, which often equates activity with accomplishment. He argues that this mindset may result in overcommitment and superficial work, ultimately causing stress and diminishing the value of one's contributions.

I'm not particularly fond of the word "slow," but many of Newport's ideas genuinely resonate with me. I highly recommend reading his book.

Limit Your Commitments

In addition to your formal responsibilities, you'll likely be constantly inundated with requests from multiple sources, including superiors, peers, and subordinates. These requests not only demand a chunk of your time but also add cognitive load. You have to worry about, discuss, clarify, execute, and deliver the work coming out of these requests.

Technological tools like email and instant messaging have significantly amplified this issue. With just a few clicks, anyone can instantly grab your attention and assign you more tasks, often without consideration for your current workload or priorities. As a result, the line between meaningful work and reactive busy work becomes blurred, leaving you juggling competing demands.

Another reason to be cautious is that we humans are notoriously poor at estimating how long intangible efforts, like knowledge work, might take to complete. We tend to imagine best-case scenarios. This tendency stems from overconfidence in our abilities and a natural inclination to underestimate the impact of unknowns, risks, and external factors that can derail our timelines.

This optimistic bias can lead to unrealistic deadlines, overcommitment, and unnecessary stress when things inevitably take longer than anticipated. If you're not selective about what you commit to, you won't have the time and mental energy to focus on what's most important. And in the worst case, it can result in you burning out.

I used to struggle with saying no to people's requests. It felt awkward and left me worried that I might come across as not being a team player. I also mistakenly believed that the more tasks I took, the more productive I would appear. This attitude often led me to work excessive overtime, including weekends, just to keep up.

Here are some strategies that can help you limit your commitments.

Publicize What You're Working On

One added benefit of being transparent with your goals, or, as we discussed earlier, OKRs, is that people can easily find out what your priorities are and how much work you have. You can use your OKRs as a shield against less important requests. If your OKRs are aligned with the organization's, you shouldn't have difficulty pushing back on work that doesn't contribute to them.

This is one of the reasons why I strongly advocate keeping the team's ongoing work visible using task management tools. Indeed, managing task tickets takes effort, but I think it's worth it in exchange for visibility. These solutions provide a centralized platform where all team members can log their tasks, update their progress, and visualize the overall workload. Visibility is invaluable for both internal team members and external stakeholders, who can effortlessly see everyone's current tasks and priorities at a glance.

You can automate reports to show what's going on from different perspectives. For example, the number of bugs being fixed, the number of new features being implemented, story points being executed by each team member, project progress, etc.

On the other hand, your organization might change priorities that merit reformulating goals. When this happens, take the time to reorient yourself and your team to align with the new objectives. Then, communicate broadly the change.

Focus on One Big Thing per Day

This suggestion is simple: You need uninterrupted lengths of time to do good work. Pick the most important, high-impact task on your plate and commit to making it your mission for the day. Either complete it or at least make tangible progress on it.

Avoiding context switching between tasks helps facilitate entering a state of flow. In his book *Flow: The Psychology of Optimal Experience*, psychologist Mihaly Csikszentmihalyi defines a state of flow as a highly focused mental state in which individuals become fully immersed and engaged in an activity. This state is characterized by a deep sense of concentration, enjoyment, and intrinsic motivation, and the person loses awareness of time and self-consciousness.

We all have experienced this. A state of deep focus, where time goes by fast and progress is quick. Csikszentmihalyi emphasizes that achieving flow facilitates optimal experiences that enhance personal growth, creativity, and overall well-being.

However, this doesn't mean it's the only thing you should do. You have other responsibilities that require your attention, such as supporting your team, attending meetings, and responding to emails and messages. These duties can't be ignored but can be managed so they don't consume your entire day.

Schedule Your Work

Use your calendar as a tool to protect and manage your time. Beyond scheduling meetings, allocate specific blocks of time for important, recurring work. Assigning these tasks to particular days and times creates a structured routine, preventing you from constantly reacting to what's urgent.

Reserving time on your calendar prevents colleagues from scheduling meetings during those slots, ensuring you have the space to focus on high-priority work without interruptions. Once you set clear boundaries on your time, people around you will likely respect them. For instance, if one of your responsibilities is reviewing architectural designs, you can schedule a 30-minute slot each week to focus exclusively on this work. Let your team know that if they want something reviewed, they should submit it by this time.

Another benefit of scheduling is that it sets clear time limits for the task, preventing it from consuming excessive time. If the work needs much more time than anticipated, it likely means you underestimated or didn't fully understand it. If this is the case, reassess its importance and schedule a different time to continue it if necessary.

Avoid Unreasonable Deadlines

I've seen individuals in a place of power set unreasonable deadlines for their teams. Their intent might be to inspire innovation, encourage creative problem-solving, and push individuals to unlock their potential. However, this approach rarely delivers the desired outcome.

When engineers are forced to work under intense time pressure, they become overconstrained, and the first thing they sacrifice is quality. They will push problems to the future or, even worse, to the user. Whatever output results from these efforts will likely have to be redone.

A common trait among those who impose unreasonable deadlines is their distance from hands-on work. They lack a deep understanding of what actually needs to be done, the complexities involved, and the trade-offs required. This disconnect is what allows them to put other people under the gun.

This is why I've made it a point to stay close to the code. Staying close to the work not only keeps me grounded but also reminds me to be empathetic to my people's challenges. It allows me to make informed decisions, set realistic expectations, and provide support when needed.

Moreover, I always expect the same from my direct reports regardless of their role. Being "in the trenches" with the team isn't just a symbolic gesture—it's an important practice. Leaders who remain connected to the work can better anticipate obstacles, identify opportunities for efficiency, and protect their teams when external pressures mount. Leadership is not about issuing directives from an ivory tower; it's about shared ownership.

When engineers are forced to sacrifice quality over delivery speed, there is a psychological negative effect: It deprives them of being proud of what they produce. Tom DeMarco and Timothy Lister write about it in their book *Peopleware: Productive Projects and Teams*: "We managers tend to think of quality as just another attribute of the product, something that may be supplied in varying degrees according to the needs of the marketplace...The builders' view of quality, on the other hand, is very different. Since their self-esteem is strongly tied to the quality of the product, they tend to impose quality standards of their own."

One could argue that imposing an unreasonable deadline on someone effectively robs them of their agency. It prevents them from having autonomy and ownership over how tasks are approached and completed because the only available option is the fastest one.

Eat Your Own Dog Food

Eating your dog food, or "dogfooding," refers to using your products or services in real-world scenarios to verify their quality, usability, and effectiveness. Nothing beats trying things out for yourself.

It makes a big difference when you're an actual user of the software you're building. It inspires you to come up with better ideas for features, examine the user experience more closely, empathize with customers, and offer firsthand feedback to your team.

I suggest promoting internal dogfooding programs that encourage everyone in your organization to use and test the software you develop actively. These programs can involve employees from various departments—including engineering, product management, design, marketing, and customer support—to get feedback from different perspectives.

When I was VP of Engineering at Drivemode, Honda's software development arm, I was responsible for building the software platform for electric motorcycles. The difference in engagement between engineers who actually rode bikes and those who didn't was striking. The former group would happily go on rides to test the software and return with plenty of feedback on improving its quality. They consistently came up with the most innovative and impactful ideas. For example, they noticed some UI elements were too distracting when glancing at the navigation guidance while riding. Others, including me, would rely on these engineers for guidance, regardless of seniority or official role. They became champions for our customers.

Being a user of your software gives you a more profound understanding of the impact of your work. I recommend looking for opportunities to work on the software you use, want to use, or at least relate with. If you get lucky, you'll find more enjoyment and naturally be more engaged in your work.

Key Points

- High-quality work stems from focused attention on fewer, high-priority tasks.

- Productivity in software engineering should measure the impact, not just output volume.

- Unrealistic deadlines often lead to poor-quality work, reduced team morale, and a loss of ownership for engineers.

- Stay connected to the work, and involve yourself in the hands-on process to set achievable expectations.

- Use your products regularly to understand their real-world impact, improve usability, and gain empathy for users.

CHAPTER 11

Take Care of Yourself

This is this book's final and most important advice: take care of yourself.

No job is worth sacrificing your physical or mental health. Burnout is very real and can leave you scarred for life. While it's okay to push yourself during critical moments—such as before a major product delivery or an important meeting—it's equally important to take breaks afterward to recover. These intense stretches should be short and never become the norm.

Some well-known symptoms to look for when you suspect you're burning out are intense stress, insomnia, lack of appetite, extreme fatigue, irritability, apathy, and lack of motivation. If you sense any of these, take a break immediately and seek professional medical help. Again, there is no shame in relying on people; on the contrary, it is a sign of bravery and commitment to the long term.

Burnout was first identified in 1974 by psychologist Herbert Freudenberger, who was studying the impact of working in a free addiction clinic on his colleagues. He described it as a state of emotional and physical exhaustion, particularly affecting healthcare workers due to the emotionally taxing and demanding nature of their jobs. Over time, the concept of burnout expanded and was applied to various other professions and industries.

© Jonathan Sosa 2025
J. Sosa, *From Culture to Code*, Apress Pocket Guides,
https://doi.org/10.1007/979-8-8688-1428-0_11

Freudenberger further developed his ideas and, in collaboration with Gail North, created the 12-stage model of burnout, which is outlined below:

1. The compulsion to prove oneself and to demonstrate worth obsessively. It tends to affect the best employees who readily accept responsibility.

2. Working harder, an inability to switch off.

3. Neglecting their needs: Erratic sleeping, eating disrupted, lack of social interaction.

4. Displacement of conflicts: Problems are dismissed, and we may feel threatened, panicky, and jittery.

5. Revision of values: Values are skewed, friends and family are dismissed, hobbies are seen as irrelevant, and work is the only focus.

6. Denial of emerging problems; intolerance, perceiving collaborators as stupid, lazy, demanding, or undisciplined, social contacts harder; cynicism, aggression; problems are viewed as caused by time pressure and work, not because of life changes.

7. Withdrawal: Social life small or nonexistent, need to feel relief from stress, with alcohol, drugs, or other damaging behavior.

8. Odd behavioral changes: Changes in behavior are obvious, and friends and family are concerned.

9. Depersonalization: Seeing neither self nor others as valuable and no longer perceive own needs.

10. Inner emptiness: Feeling empty inside, and to overcome this, look for activities such as overeating, sex, alcohol, or drugs; activities are often exaggerated.

11. Depression: Feeling lost and unsure, exhausted; future feels bleak and dark.

12. Total mental and physical collapse.

I'm sure some of these ring a bell for you. Everyone in a leadership position has experienced some level of burnout to get to where they are. Status comes with a hefty price; just don't let it become too costly.

Burnout doesn't just affect you—it also affects your family and friends. Taking care of your well-being is not only a personal responsibility but also a way to guarantee you can be there for the people you love. Workplace stress almost always bleeds into home life. Your family will notice your lack of energy, your irritability, or your absence of enthusiasm for things.

You can always find a new job, but not a new family.

I've come close to burning out twice in my career. The first time was right after the Lehman Brothers collapse in 2008. Like many others, the company I worked for lost most of its customers and didn't have enough money to make payroll. I vividly remember the CEO coming to my house on the weekend to apologize and handing me a portion of my salary that was already a month overdue.

During these hard times, I was working like crazy. I was still young, but the sheer workload, combined with the stress of not knowing if I would be paid, started to take a toll. My mind wouldn't let me rest—it was constantly racing, trying to find solutions and make sense of the uncertainty.

Eventually, I decided to consult a doctor. They diagnosed me with anxiety-related stress and warned that if I continued down this path, I could fall into a deep depression. I took a monthlong leave, allowing myself the time to recover fully. That break was essential in helping me regain my health and clarity. I returned to work and ended up becoming the CTO.

The second time I came close to burning out was in 2019. I led the development of a new C2C ecommerce feature for the Mercari mobile app. I was spending, on average, 12 hours a day in the office, driven by a strong sense of motivation. Having recently joined the company, I was eager to make a positive impression and build a strong reputation. But it was simply too much work, and the deadline was too aggressive. Fortunately, the project was delivered before it started to take a serious toll on my health.

On both occasions, I was single and living alone. Now that I have a wife and daughter, the thought of working long hours away from them feels unimaginable. I don't want to miss out on important life moments or bring unnecessary stress into our home. Knowing my obsessive tendencies make it difficult to disconnect from work, I've committed to avoid putting myself in those situations again.

I've learned to take work slightly less seriously. I still work overtime often, but I also force myself to take breaks, exercise almost every morning, go out on walks, and take time to do the things I love outside my profession. I know I'm in a privileged position, and not everyone has the luxury to say "no" to their boss and reserve time for themselves. But I urge you to care for yourself and those close to you.

CHAPTER 12

Closing Words

That was a lot, wasn't it?

Fortunately, you don't need to excel at everything—no one can. Each of us has our own strengths and weaknesses. Personally, I have high levels of empathy and tend to avoid conflict, so dealing with low performers and delivering negative feedback is particularly stressful for me. I need to take ample time to prepare for these situations, carefully collecting, documenting, and polishing the feedback before giving it.

I'm sure you're aware of your limitations. Acknowledging them is a sign of strength, not weakness. It's perfectly acceptable to seek support from your team, peers, and superiors when needed. You can also bring external resources, like management and leadership training or technical consultants, to help you.

If you're someone who hesitates to ask for help, consider this: by learning from the experiences of others, you're effectively leveraging the time and effort they've already invested in mastering the same subject. Instead of starting from scratch, you can build upon their knowledge, which saves you time and helps you avoid potential pitfalls they may have encountered.

Forget your ego and put your people first. Their success and careers depend on how effective a leader you are. Even if they leave the organization and become leaders themselves somewhere else, they'll never forget what they learned from you. Be the person that everyone wants to work with.

© Jonathan Sosa 2025
J. Sosa, *From Culture to Code*, Apress Pocket Guides,
https://doi.org/10.1007/979-8-8688-1428-0_12

Nothing brings me greater satisfaction than learning that a former team member has advanced in their career and is now leading their own team. Witnessing their professional growth and knowing I may have contributed to their development is incredibly rewarding. Some engineers I worked with years ago have progressed to hold prestigious positions such as Director, Vice President, and even Chief Technology Officer.

Their accomplishments inspire me to continue investing in others, nurturing talent, and creating opportunities for growth in my current position. Ultimately, their success is a testament to the positive impact we can have on each other's careers when we work together and support one another. This is what being a multiplier is all about.

That's it. Whether you began reading this book with the goal of becoming a better engineering leader or seeking clarity on how to step into such a role, I hope you have gained insights and are inspired to put them into practice. Information holds little value without action, so I encourage you to pick and implement the two or three ideas that resonate most with you. Perhaps you can formulate a few personal OKRs to work on them.

I also hope that this becomes a resource you can refer to time and time again whenever you're faced with a new challenge. Some of my suggestions may only fully make sense once you're in the specific situation they address. As you encounter different scenarios, you'll likely find that the advice here becomes more relevant.

The content of this book will evolve as I continue to learn and collect experiences. I'm looking forward to your feedback. Please visit **https:// fromculturetocode.com** and share your thoughts.

Thank you for joining me on this journey. Embrace the challenges ahead, celebrate your successes, and remember that leadership is a continuous learning experience. Wishing you all the best in your endeavors.

Jonathan

Bibliography

Scott Eblin, *The Next Level: What Insiders Know About Executive Success* (Nicholas Brealey, 2010).

Harvard Business Review, *Manager's Handbook* (Harvard Business Review Press, 2017).

Janice Fraser, *Farther, Faster and Far Less Drama: How to Reduce Stress and Make Extraordinary Progress Wherever You Lead* (Matt Holt Books, 2023).

Jim Collins, *Good to Great: Why Some Companies Make the Leap, And Others Don't* (Harper Business, 2011).

Matthew Skelton and Manuel Pais, *Team Topologies: Organizing Business and Technology Teams for Fast Flow* (IT Revolution Press, 2019).

Ernest O'Boyle Jr., Herman Aguinis, *The Best and the Rest: Revisiting the Norm of Normality of Individual Performance* (Kelley School of Business, 2012).

John Doerr, *Measure What Matters: How Google, Bono, and the Gates Foundation Rock the World with OKRs* (Portfolio, 2018).

Jason Fried and David Heinemeier, *Rework* (Crown Business, 2010).

Erin Meyer, *The Culture Map: Breaking Through the Invisible Boundaries of Global Business* (PublicAffairs, 2016).

Terese Besker, Antonio Martini, and Jan Bosch, *Software Developer Productivity Loss Due to Technical Debt* (2019).

Cal Newport, *Slow Productivity: The Lost Art of Accomplishment Without Burnout* (Portfolio, 2024).

Mihaly Csikszentmihalyi, *Flow: The Psychology of Optimal Experience* (HarperCollins, 2008).

Tom DeMarco, Timothy Lister, *Peopleware: Productive Projects and Teams* (Addison-Wesley Professional, 2013).

© Jonathan Sosa 2025
J. Sosa, *From Culture to Code*, Apress Pocket Guides,
https://doi.org/10.1007/979-8-8688-1428-0

GPSR Compliance
The European Union's (EU) General Product Safety Regulation (GPSR) is a set
of rules that requires consumer products to be safe and our obligations to
ensure this.

If you have any concerns about our products, you can contact us on

ProductSafety@springernature.com

In case Publisher is established outside the EU, the EU authorized
representative is:

Springer Nature Customer Service Center GmbH
Europaplatz 3
69115 Heidelberg, Germany